To Fred
Best wishes Always
Hank Failer

Best wishes, Fred!
It great meeting you in
Williamsburg —
Sincerely
Doug Williams

A Pirate's Journey

The Life Story of Major League Catcher Hank Foiles

with Douglas Williams

Editor: Susan Pongratz
Cover design: Mike O'Reilly
Photo editor: Mike O'Reilly
Endorsements by: Dick Groat
Bill Mazeroski
Bob Friend

Photographs: Used with permission, from the Hank Foiles family collection and the Douglas Williams collection

Trademarks, logos and other photographs, used with permission from the Pittsburgh Pirates National League Baseball Club

ISBN 978-0-7414-6897-0
Library of Congress Control Number: 2011939029

Printed in the United States of America

Published December 2011

INFINITY PUBLISHING
1094 New DeHaven Street, Suite 100
West Conshohocken, PA 19428-2713
Toll-free (877) BUY BOOK
Local Phone (610) 941-9999
Fax (610) 941-9959
Info@buybooksontheweb.com
www.buybooksontheweb.com

ACKNOWLEDGMENTS

Throughout the course of our lives, each of us has drawn our own conclusions about things like prosperity and success. While too many of us see material riches and money as indicators of success, I believe that a truly successful life is attainable through other means, like reaching our goals in life and finding happiness in our work, through our relationships and our families. By my own standards, I believe I have enjoyed a successful and rewarding life and that I still have a few exciting innings yet to play. Over the years I have been blessed through countless friendships and have reaped the benefits of having wonderful parents and a beautiful family of my own.

Vince Lombardi was on course when he told his players, "The only place you'll find where success comes before work is in the dictionary." And in keeping with his viewpoint, I can truly say that I accomplished a lot in life through my own blood, sweat and tears and a lot of hard work. However, that is not to say that I did it all alone.

The list of people who have helped me along the way is much too long for me to name each one individually, so I will not attempt to do so. Yet so many people have believed in me, encouraged me, trusted me, supported me and tolerated me throughout my life, that I am overwhelmed by the number. To each of you I offer my sincere gratitude for the role you played in making my life what it is today.

To my wife, Joyce, I owe so very much. She has been my wall, standing beside me without fail since we were teenagers. She has given me love and support through the good times and the bad, holding her tongue and forcing herself to listen to me when I had nothing but complaints. I will always treasure those rare occasions when she snapped back and put me in my place, causing me to realize that even she could take only so much. For instance, there was that time in Pittsburgh, when I came home fuming, mired in a dreadful batting slump and she tried her best to console me. My inconsiderate response to her kindly efforts was to advise her to "tend to the cooking and leave the hitting to me!" I'll never forget how quickly she got to the bottom of my problem and told me exactly what I needed to hear, "If I cook as poorly as you hit, we'll all starve to death!" she shouted back. It was funny to see how quickly my batting average began to climb back up, starting with my very next game!

I am forever grateful to my parents for the nurturing and guidance they gave me, particularly the well-structured advice of my father and the discipline of my mother. It was Daddy who showed me how to believe in myself and how to deal with the issues of life, while it was Momma who taught me to attend church, believe in God and to respect others.

I extend loving appreciation to my sons, Hank (Henry L. Foiles III) and Marc (Marc L. Foiles), for understanding me and for the closeness we enjoy today. I am aware of how it can be trying at times for each of you to be my son, but I want you to know that it has been through my demands and expectations that I have wanted only the best for you. I am proud of the men you have become and delighted by the successes you have each found in your chosen fields of work.

Shirley (Shirley Lee Foiles Owens) is my loving and protective sister who, since my earliest memories, has always been there for me. As a brother, I appreciate all the guidance she has given me over the years.

It was my cousin, Roy (Roy Burton Jr.), who was as close to me as any brother could have been. It was Roy, my willing mentor, who not only encouraged me, but inspired me and always set a wonderful example for me to follow. Roy, I'm still looking up to you.

Finally, I send special thanks to those who turned this idea of writing a book into a reality. I wish to recognize my co-author, Doug Williams, our editor, Susan Pongratz, and our photo editor/graphics designer, Mike O'Reilly, for their many hours of hard work. Thanks to everyone, it's been a great experience and a lot of fun.

DEDICATION

In loving memory of my parents,
Henry Lee Foiles Sr.
And
Nellie Morton Foiles
Together they gave me the ideal combination of love, support, discipline and guidance.

TABLE OF CONTENTS

FOREWORD

It's hard to imagine just how long ago it really was, but the decade of the 1960s was a great time to grow up. For our country it was a decade of great social and political change, but one of economic prosperity as well. In 1962, the average American household saw an increase in income of 4% to about $6,000 per year, the result of a robust economy that gave most families the means to afford at least one automobile, a telephone and a television set. Ownership of these relatively new luxuries meant that American families were seeing more of the U.S.A. in their Chevrolet, letting their fingers do the walking through the Yellow Pages and kindly dropping in on Uncle Jed and the Clampett family on CBS every Wednesday night.

Yet, in addition to these high-dollar commodities which benefited the entire family, there were other new trendy items for us kids which were more than just signs of prosperous times. These were accessories needed to reach certain levels of social acceptance. For example, your battery-powered, portable radio had to be at least an eight transistor model with an ear plug and a leather case if you wanted to be hip when you tuned in to hear The Beach Boys or The Four Seasons. Moreover, your chances were good for being a finalist as the most envied boy in the neighborhood if you came coasting by on a shiny new Schwinn bike with the stylish new Slim-Line Tank. You could possibly turn a few heads in the school lunchroom if your Thermos lunch box was emblazoned with pictures of Lucas McCain, The Rifleman, or maybe Dodge City's most famous lawman, Marshall Matt Dillon

On the other hand, a boy's baseball glove could also be a make or break item when it came to playground status. Factors that were up for consideration included the size of the glove. Was it a kid's model or large enough for an older boy? And what about the manufacturer? A mitt made by Wilson, Hutch or Rawlings, or any glove good enough to be pictured in *Boy's Life* was okay, especially if it bore the endorsement of a famous star player. While names like Mickey Mantle, Roger Maris and Al Kaline would draw the most attention, a glove with the approval of any big leaguer was usually enough to make you an early pick when it was time to choose up sides on the sandlot.

In November 1962, during the days leading up to my tenth birthday, I could hardly contain my excitement as I had already asked my mom and dad for a catcher's mitt and I was confident they would do everything possible to keep from disappointing me. For days I had been poring over my baseball cards, separating the catchers from the rest of the collection for a closer look at their mitts. The excitement and anticipation had me day dreaming as I closely examined those precious rectangles of cardboard. *Would my catcher's mitt resemble the one Del Rice used or would it be closer to the styles of Charlie Lau or Clay Dalrymple?*

You can imagine how excited I was when the big day finally arrived. My unbridled delight was at its peak when I recklessly tore into my birthday package and found a Rawlings official Hank Foiles professional model catcher's mitt! It was beautiful! The leather was stiff and rigid and the smell told me it was newly oiled. It fit my hand perfectly. I had no doubt that after getting it broken-in over the winter, I would be a catcher in high demand by the time spring rolled around. I would be ready for games on the playground at school, around the neighborhood in the afternoons and even for imaginary games by myself in the backyard. I had visions of being a catcher in Little League and Pony League and even pondered whether or not I should use this same mitt when the time came for me to break into the pros!

I went back to my hoard of pasteboards, stashed away in a shoebox under my bed and pulled out the only Hank Foiles card I could find, a 1961 Topps. And as if it were magic, that card suddenly became my favorite. Of the more than 200 baseball and football cards bound by rubber bands and stored in that box, it was that particular one that was quickly transformed into the one with the highest importance. I studied the stats and the short biography on the back of the card. I learned that Mr. Foiles, while regarded as a fine defensive catcher, batted .282 the previous year and smashed a pinch-hit single in the 1957 All-Star game. And as if those little interesting tid-bits of baseball knowledge weren't enough to make me proud to have his name on my new mitt, then this other subsequent piece of information from the reverse of the card would clinch it for me. His home was in nearby Norfolk, Virginia!

Then, before I even had a chance to find out that Elston Howard had been traded to the Boston Red Sox, the years went flying past. They flew by like dry brittle leaves caught up in a late October gust. And while my hand grew to be a little too big to slip easily in and out of my Hank Foiles model catcher's mitt, my love of baseball and my passion for collecting memorabilia associated with the game never waned. It was through my fervent collecting of baseball autographs that I became connected with Mr. Foiles in an amazing way that resulted in a great friendship as well as in the writing of this book.

Even after approaching him for autographs at several local hobby shows in the 1980s, it wasn't until 1995 that I took a close look at some of the items in my collection and noticed that his name was missing from an autographed baseball signed by members of the 1955 Cleveland Indians. After digging through the record books and finding that Mr. Foiles had appeared in 62 games for the Tribe that season, I realized that he was too close by to not have his signature on the ball, along with so many of his teammates. I wasn't aware of any upcoming public signings or shows that had him scheduled as an autograph guest, so I decided to take matters into my own hands.

Knowing only that he lived in the Southside area of Tidewater and that he worked many years in his own insurance and financial business, I set out to do some detective work. I picked up the phone and began my search, dialing similar Norfolk based businesses listed in the local phone book. After three or four calls, a helpful lady working at a financial firm was kind enough to provide me with a company name, a phone number and an address for Mr. Foiles's office, which was located only a few blocks away from her place. In minutes I had the former catcher on the line. He listened patiently as I explained my situation and my purpose for tracking him down. I found him to be friendly and receptive. He even suggested that I drive over to Norfolk to meet with him in his office later that afternoon. He also urged me to bring along any of my other collectibles that needed his signature and he'd be happy to accommodate me.

My visit with him that afternoon was a memorable one. He signed my Indians baseball and a few other pieces, including my old Rawlings catcher's mitt, with his imprinted name still bold and legible after so many years. Yet, he had a lot more to offer than just his signature. He had memories to share which centered on some of his Cleveland teammates whose names were already on the ball. He told me funny stories about Bob Feller packing dumbbells in his suitcases for road trips and how a young left-handed fireballer named

Herb Score would sometimes sail his fastballs against the backstop, striking the screen some 15 feet above the ground! He spoke about the time he helped an airline stewardess serve a mid-air dinner and drinks to his Pittsburgh Pirate teammates and how, in the only major league game that his father would see him play, he went 2 for 3 at the plate to help defeat the Yankees in Cleveland.

He also introduced me to his son, Marc, who was working alongside his father, there in the office. Marc, a personable, outgoing fellow about my age, was a pleasure to meet. He was quick to talk about his work in the financial field as well as his interests outside the office. Like me, he enjoys sports, music and antiques, which provided enough common ground to connect us as good friends from the start.

In 2005, I wrote about my relationship with Hank and Marc and my old catcher's mitt in my first book, *So Many Summer Fields*. I wrote about my ongoing friendship with Marc and a few other short baseball stories about Hank. However, it is the subtitle of that book that so appropriately applies to my meeting these two men. The subtitle, *Creating Friendships While Connecting to Baseball's Past* is the perfect summation for what has developed since my visit to their office.

While I believe that I did a satisfactory job of writing about Hank and his experiences in my earlier book, I began to realize that the more I got to know him, the more I came to see just how compelling and complex his life has been. Through the years of our friendship, I found that the more stories he told, the more there were left for him to tell. His past experiences as a high school athlete, a pro baseball player, a husband, a father, a grandfather, a Masonic brother and a trusted friend are far too fascinating and entertaining to let slip away.

The life and career of Hank Foiles cannot be depicted in a full book, much less in just one short chapter, yet he and I have given it our best shot. By culling through his endless stockpile of stories, we have attempted to provide you, the reader, with an accurate account of what it was like for a boy, born at the onset of the Great Depression, to realize his dream of playing baseball in the major leagues. It is also our intent to show how pro baseball can be an exciting and rewarding life, while there are also days filled with uncertainty and disappointment. We hoped to tell how injuries, player transactions, team politics, unscrupulous general managers and other factors can sometimes sour a career in baseball. In various ways we have pointed out how Hank has seen the game change both positively and negatively over the years, while still maintaining our common belief that baseball is the greatest game of them all.

So, I ask myself… *How did this all come to be? Why is it, that I am blessed to have the opportunity to work with Mr. Foiles on his autobiography? And how is it that we became such good friends?* All the while, I am often asked by others if I believe this whole arrangement was predetermined or just simply one of those things that was "meant to be." In Psalm 16:11 David wrote; "Thou wilt show me the path of life." Now, looking back almost a half century, I see how a catcher's mitt given to me by my parents could well have been a symbol suggesting my life's path, possibly giving me a subtle glimpse into my future, but arriving at a time when I was too young to see it. Today, my reward is seeing how it all fell into place so many years later.

Douglas Williams
August 2011

HANK
FOILES

CHAPTER 1

TOUCHING A DISTANT STAR

The weather was stifling. The combination of heat and humidity was enough to take your breath but what else could you expect on a summer afternoon in St. Louis? It was July 9, 1957. The scene was Sportsman's Park, and the event was the 24th Major League All-Star Game. The hot, sticky conditions were nothing more than minor incidentals for the players and the 31,000 fans that squeezed their way in. Most of the paying customers were from right there in the local area, mid-westerners who were dyed-in-the-wool Cardinal fans. On this day, however, they were all rooters for the stars of the National League and their allegiance was being put to the test. The American Leaguers had inflicted just enough damage to keep a lid on the crowd's enthusiasm by scoring twice in the second inning and once again in the sixth. The traditional seventh inning stretch had been the only reason for the fans to rise to their feet as the A.L. pitchers had dominated the game to this point. It wasn't until Gus Bell of the Cincinnati Reds drove in a pair of runs in the bottom of the seventh that we got on the scoreboard and cut the lead to 3-2. Other than tipping my cap to the crowd during the pre-game introductions, my only duties of the afternoon had been to grab my mitt and warm up a couple of our relief pitchers.

Don't get me wrong, it was a great honor for me to be named to the National League All-Star squad, but spending my day in the bullpen was particularly difficult knowing that my numbers were the best among all N.L. catchers going into the midseason break. This made me even more anxious to get into the game and hopefully strike a much-needed spark to help get our offense going. Other than my manager, Bobby Bragan, who was serving as a N.L. coach, I was the only representative from the Pittsburgh Pirates on a squad that was chocked full of Cincinnati players. Fan voting has always been a fun part of the mid-summer classic, but for this particular season the election process had gotten a little out of hand. Reds fans did a lot more than their share by stuffing the ballot boxes for their hometown favorites. This voting frenzy resulted in a National League starting lineup, which featured eight position players, all from Cincinnati! Fortunately, the Commissioner of Baseball, Ford Frick, stepped in and inserted a few of our circuit's superstars from other clubs to provide some needed diversity and balance.

The A.L. struck again in the top of the ninth inning, adding three more runs. They found a way to bunch together a couple of singles and a double and took advantage of an infield error to extend their lead to 6-2. To make matters worse, the Americans had gone to their bullpen for southpaw, Billy Pierce of the Chicago White Sox, who had been in complete control since he entered the game in the seventh. It was as if he had used a shiny coin, swinging back and forth on the end of a string, to lull our hitters into a lethargic trance. He retired the first five batters he faced without allowing a ball to leave the infield. However, things were about to change abruptly as he discovered his hypnotic skills were no longer effective in the bottom of the ninth inning.

Once I noticed Pierce, a lefthander, had taken the mound for the A.L., I figured my chances of getting called into the game as a pinch-batter increased considerably. Reds' catcher Ed Bailey, a lefty batter, had played the entire afternoon, so I saw myself as a possible late inning replacement. I was also hopeful for an opportunity to face Pierce because of my past experience with him, when as a member of the Cleveland ball club, I squared off against him with successful results many times in the American League. Yet, I would still need to wait and see what our skipper, Walt Alston, would choose to do. He still had a few potent batters left on his roster, including one of his own right-handed power hitters from the Dodgers, Gil Hodges.

A hearty round of applause erupted from the stands when Stan "The Man" Musial made his way toward the plate to lead off the bottom of the ninth. As the Cardinal great and hometown favorite took his final swings before stepping into the batter's box, some of the other players in our bullpen were frantically clamoring for my attention. They all wanted me to catch the signal coming from the bench. One of our players in the dugout was standing on the top step staring intently in the direction of the bullpen. First, he waved his arms above his head to get noticed. Next, he placed his hands together in front of his chest, and with palms outward, placed the tips of his thumbs together. In the language of traditional baseball charades, it was understood that this signal meant the catcher was being called for duty. That call was for me!

I wasted no time, hopping up and jogging along the left field foul line, past third base and on to the dugout. As I started down the steps and headed in the direction of the bat rack, an unidentified voice yelled to me.

"Grab your bat, Hank, you're in the hole! You're hitting for Bailey!"

After a quick scan of the rack, I spotted my bat with my identifying mark, #20, on the end of the knob. As I pulled it from its pigeonhole, I heard another round of applause come from the stands as Musial had coaxed a base on balls..

In spite of holding a four-run lead and having allowed only one runner to reach base, Billy Pierce was about to enter a danger zone into which no pitcher would want to venture. His predicament was quickly turning into a pitcher's worst nightmare. His next opponent was none other than "The Say Hey Kid," Willie Mays!

I slowly trudged my way back up the dugout steps to ground level and began to swing my bat, first in small circular rotations above my head and then as I stopped in midstride, I took a couple of full level swings across my body.

If Willie gets on base, this game could get interesting. If he gets a base hit here, I'll have a great opportunity to make a difference in this game.

I stepped into the circle with my bat across my right shoulder and dropped to one knee. I snatched up the rosin bag and gave my hands and wrists a liberal dusting of the course, powdery substance. Lots of rosin was a requirement on a day like this if I hoped to keep my grip on the slippery handle of that bat. This was the All-Star Game, so I wanted to have every advantage I could get.

Pierce continued to work from a set position, so with the crafty left-hander facing directly towards him, Musial took a cautious lead away from the bag. I glanced back over toward Mays just in time to see him take an inside-out swing at Pierce's next offering and drive it down the right field line and into the corner. There, the baseball ricocheted like a pinball off the outfield wall and into the area of the A.L. bullpen. Willie finally came to a stop at third base with a stand-up triple, driving in Musial all the way from first! Willie's RBI hit closed the gap to 6-3 and left us in a good position to mount a comeback. We now had a runner on third and still there were no outs.

I rose to my feet and began to take a step or two in the direction of the batter's box. As an afterthought, I turned back and tossed the rosin bag back into the circle. I advanced toward the plate with the voice of confidence telling me I could handle this job as well as anyone.

And why shouldn't I? I reassured myself. There were others as well, who were showing confidence in me at this very moment. In particular, there was my manager, Walter Alston, who had other pinch-hitting options. He still had some big guns remaining in his arsenal, yet he called on me to come through with a clutch hit and to keep the rally going. And sure, this was a very critical point in one of the biggest baseball games of the year, but I thrived on pressure. I loved it! In past seasons, I had been put in tough situations like this many times and often I managed to deliver a key hit. I was always mindful of the pressure, yet I was aware that it was being felt on both sides, by the pitcher as well as the batter. In just a brief flashing moment I recalled a bit of advice that was given to me by the great Joe DiMaggio. I was attending my first professional spring training camp as a young Yankee farmhand when the Yankee Clipper imparted to me some valuable words of wisdom.

"Always remember, Hank," he offered. "maintain confidence in yourself and know for a fact, that the other guy had to put his pants on the same way you did…one leg at a time!"

I stepped into the batter's box just as the public address announcer finished introducing me as a pinch hitter. With the spikes of my right shoe, I began to scrape away some of the bright orange clay, digging a small crease in the dirt for my back foot. I sensed a degree of familiarity as I looked out to the mound and saw Pierce again go to his set position. We had faced each other many times before, but never in such a crucial situation. This time things were different; he appeared to be rattled and uneasy. But maybe he had a just cause, as he stepped off the pitching rubber and glared over at Mays who was daringly extending his lead away from third base. Undoubtedly, Pierce was about to work himself into a pickle.

His first pitch came in high and fast. It was obvious that catcher Yogi Berra had called for something different like, perhaps a curveball that would break downward into the strike zone. Like a rocket, this fastball sailed past me about head high and barely nicked the tip of Yogi's mitt on its flight towards the backstop! Seeing that Yogi had no chance to recover the wild pitch in time, I quickly sprung backwards, away from the plate and frantically waved to Willie, to let him know that the way was clear for him to come home to score. But, my signal to Willie was not really vital to the play. At the very instant the ball nicked Yogi's glove, Willie was already about a third of the way down the baseline and heading for home. He had again put his incredible base-running instincts to good use and scored standing up, long before the elusive baseball had rolled to a stop! Even though Pierce's wild pitch cleared the bases, the American League's lead had been reduced to 6-4. We definitely had their ace lefthander on the ropes and our next job was to deliver a knockout blow. There's an old baseball proverb that claims "no lead is a safe lead" and this adage should assume an even stronger tone when it is applied to a Major League All-Star game.

After seeing what Mays did with a pitch on the inside part of the plate, I thought it very unlikely that I would see any pitches in that same location. But, to my liking I got practically the same offering. The next pitch from Pierce was a fastball that once again found its way to the inner half of the plate. With a slicing swing, I managed to drive the ball the opposite way, over the head of second baseman Nellie Fox and into right-center field for a base hit! Mickey Mantle, the A.L. center fielder, scooted over to cut the ball off and threw it back to the infield. By getting on base, I had done my job, which was to simply keep the rally going and give our club a chance to get back into the game.

Casey Stengel, manager for the American League, left Pierce on the mound long enough to toss four cheap pitches high and away from out next hitter, Gus Bell. The walk allowed us to have the tying run on base, with one of the games most feared left-handed batters, Eddie Mathews of the Milwaukee Braves due up next. With the game hanging in the balance, Stengel made a counter move and resorted to his bullpen, calling in another left-handed reliever, my former Cleveland teammate, Don Mossi. With a mixture of sweeping curves and some well-located fastballs, Mossi put Mathews down with a called third strike for the first out of the inning. The Americans were still a far cry from being off the hook, as our batting order afforded them no soft touches. The National League's next hitter, "Mr. Cub," Ernie Banks, scorched a hard grounder through the hole at shortstop and into left field for a base hit. Once the ball reached the outfield grass, it appeared to slow down quickly, forcing left fielder Minnie Minoso to race in to make the play. Before Minoso could scoop up the ball and get off a throw to the plate, I rounded third base and scored easily. However, prior to the end of the play, Gus Bell derailed our chances for a comeback by attempting to advance all the way to third on the hit by Banks. It took a great throw by Minoso to third baseman Frank Malzone to nail Bell, but that's exactly what Minnie delivered and Bell was thrown out by a step.

With two outs, manager Alston again went to his bench and called on one of his own stars from the Brooklyn Dodgers, Gil Hodges, to pinch-hit for pitcher, Clem Labine. We still had a good chance to pull this game out of the fire and the sellout crowd knew it. They rose to their feet as Hodges was announced. The humid Missouri air was filled with still more tension as Banks was now in scoring position at second, after advancing on Minoso's throw.

Hodges, who was among the best run producers in the league, was a great selection for Alston to make in this situation. However, Stengle and his coaching staff were fully aware of the long ball threat he presented. So the Americans continued with the chess game-like strategy by bringing in New York Yankee right-hander Bob Grim.

Hodges swung at a pitch to his liking from Grim, but his bat got under the ball by just the slightest bit, causing him to drive a high fly ball out to left field. Minoso moved in a few steps to make the catch, for the final out, putting the finishing touch on a disappointing 6-5 loss to the American League.

After the game, our clubhouse, by contrast, was as different as night and day to that of the winning team. While the stars of the American League were celebrating their narrow escape in a noisy room packed with league dignitaries and throngs of reporters, our clubhouse had attracted far fewer sportswriters and fewer microphones and cameras. Ours was definitely a quieter, more subdued atmosphere. Each of us, as representatives of the National League, was disappointed and aware that we let ourselves down as well as our league and especially our fans. Of course, we were all looking forward to getting out of St. Louis and leaving the dreadfully hot weather behind, but it had been a wonderful experience and it was an honor and a thrill to be chosen to participate in this special game and to be a part of all of the great festivities.

Today, it is with a tremendous amount of pride that I can look back at that All-Star Game and recall a special day when I took the field with the greatest baseball players of that time. I was placed in the batting order that included some of the biggest stars ever to play the game and I was fortunate to have contributed to my team's efforts in what will always be remembered as one of the most exciting All-Star games ever played. In spite of coming out on the losing end, I took away a feeling of accomplishment, and an assurance that I had finally made it to the top of my profession. It had been the most incredible experience of my life. I was anxious to share it all with many people who were close to me, including my teammates on the Pittsburgh Pirates, my friends back home in Virginia and especially my family. At the same time, I felt a strange emptiness and a particularly strong urge to share this memorable experience with a special member of my family, one who was no longer with me.

As is the case with sons the world over, we often go through life searching for ways to gain approval from our fathers. One of the greatest honors for a young man is seeing that his father is proud of him for the things he has done as well as for the person he has become. My late father was an exceptional man, one who always found a way to provide for his family even in the most difficult times. He was also a baseball man with many years as both a player in the professional leagues and as an umpire. He was the kind of father who would have beamed with pride seeing his son receive such honors and recognition for playing a game both of us loved.

The more I think about it, he might very well have been filled with pride as I went to bat that hot afternoon in St. Louis. Perhaps he even applauded when I rounded third base and came in to score.

CHAPTER 2

WE WERE POOR BUT DIDN'T KNOW IT!

Hard times had hit America. It was the 1930s, a decade of shortages and hardships for just about everyone in the country. Jobs of any kind were hard to come by, while food, money, housing and all material goods were in short supply. For many American men, keeping the title of family breadwinner required a lot ingenuity and resourcefulness. What few employment opportunities there were often required traveling to another town or state and those scarce jobs were often low paying and temporary.

More than anything else, I guess it was my young age that kept me unaware of the financial plight of my family during this time, so the struggles we faced as a family never seemed to impact me personally. My father, through various ways, always managed to keep us afloat. I was never sure about some of the means and resources he used to keep himself gainfully employed, but at home we always appeared to have enough of the necessities to get by. During my childhood, we were never close enough for me to know him well, yet I always respected him as a father figure and for the type of man he was. It is difficult for me to look back over the years and recognize how certain people and particular events helped shape me into the person I became. However, in the case of my father, there is little doubt about the influence he had on me throughout my life. He was a man with very little free time on his hands; yet he often managed to squeeze in a game of catch with me on the lot across the street. He also found time to attend practically all of my games when I participated in high school athletics, regardless of the sport. And it was always clear that my daddy raised me to play baseball, so naturally, we would take along our gloves and a ball whenever we went to the beach. There were times he would get tickets for us to see a ball game at nearby Bain Field, the home ball park of the New York Yankees farm team, the Norfolk Tars. As a rule, Daddy usually didn't have much to say, but I knew I could count on him for his interest and support. And even if he was not aware, I learned so much from him just by watching.

My father was truly a baseball man at heart. As a young man, his passion for the game led him to many small town ball fields in the Tidewater area of Virginia and into coastal North Carolina. He played primarily as a first baseman for several area semi-pro teams until he earned offers to play professionally. Of the stops he made as a pro player, the times he played for his native town Portsmouth, Virginia, were certainly among the most rewarding seasons of his career. His baseball talents were never enough to carry him above the lower ranks of pro baseball, yet he continued to follow his heart and remained in the game long after his playing days were over. My father knew the game of baseball inside and out, to the extent that he eventually served as manager of the Hertford, North Carolina, professional club and later found acclaim working in various leagues as an umpire. His days in baseball were finished prior to my birth, so even now, many of the particulars concerning his career remain sketchy and incomplete. Nonetheless, the few baseball tales I was able to get him to share with me were stories that I found to be quite fascinating.

A baseball man at heart, my father had the ideal physique and quickness to play just about any position on the field.

It was during World War I that Dad was inducted into the United Sates Army where he quickly advanced to the rank of sergeant. No doubt, his baseball skills played a key part in keeping him stateside, as he was stationed at Camp Lee in Petersburg, Virginia, for the duration of the war. It was at this military base, which is now known as Fort Lee, that he played on the camp's baseball team and befriended another ball-playing soldier, Molly Craft, a pitcher from the Washington Senators. Like my father, Craft was also a native of Portsmouth who had experience in professional baseball. However, Molly had the distinction of making it all the way to the major leagues as well as the good fortune of having had Washington's great pitching legend Walter Johnson as his teammate.

Though I never had an opportunity to see Dad play baseball, I can imagine he was very athletic and quite agile. At almost six feet tall and weighing about 170 pounds, he had the ideal physique and quickness to play just about any position on the field. This made it easy for me to believe his claim that he once played an entire season at first base without committing an error!

Many years later, when he doled out some stern advice about playing baseball, he had only one rule for me.

"Never be a catcher, son," he ordered. "Choose any position on the field that you would like to play, except catcher. Never be a catcher!"

His words of wisdom fell only on deaf ears.

As his hitch in the Army was winding down, Dad was granted an opportunity to enroll in the officer's candidate training school, a virtual open door to big promotions and a lifetime career in the service. But, after making a quick summation of his situation, he concluded that the training school and military life was not the way for him to go. He confided to his family, friends and army buddies that the life of uniforms, repetitive drills and countless rules and regulations was not for him.

"I've had enough *squad left!* and *squad right!*" he declared. So he soon made his return to civilian life.

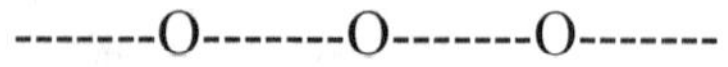

I was born the third child to Henry Lee Foiles and Nellie O'Denhall Morton in Richmond, Virginia, on June 10, 1929. I was no more than about three, maybe four years old when my mother, father and older sister Shirley packed our belongings and left Richmond with hopes of finding a better life for our family. Our destination was only about 85 miles to the southeast, in nearby Norfolk. I have practically no memories of our life in Richmond or any recollections about the reason for our move. However, it is surely safe to say that the move was in some way related to my father's search for work, as this was the early 1930s. It was the peak of The Great Depression.

Our first home in the Norfolk area was a rented house in the Estabrook neighborhood in what was then part of old Norfolk County. We were there for only about a year when it was time to pull up stakes again and move about three miles east to the Park Place section of the city. There we made our home on the first floor of a six-family apartment building on the 200 Block of West 26th Street.

After another year or two, it was time to move again. This time it was only a couple of blocks away to West 27th Street, and what an unusual move it was. Our new place was so close by that we were able to carry many of our smaller items in our arms or in boxes. For larger items, I put my Radio Flyer wagon to good use and made many trips across the street and down the sidewalk hauling everything from clothes to small furniture and heavier boxes.

I was almost six years old when we finally settled in the Park Place neighborhood of Norfolk, in our new residence at 217 West 27th Street. At the time Park Place was the kind of neighborhood where everyone felt safe and comfortable. The peaceful sights and delightful sounds of the area were enough to make anyone want to call the place home. The people there were all very friendly; and everyone seemed to know one another.

I can't come up with a definite reason for the warm familiarity that existed among our neighbors, but the folks of Park Place knew the names of those who lived next door as well as the family that lived in the house across the street. Maybe it was because people spent a lot more time outside than they do today. Maybe, as a society, we are victims of our own technological advances. As I was growing up, the folks of the neighborhood spent their spring and summer evenings outside, sitting on their front porches, fanning and waiting to catch an occasional breeze. Perhaps they enjoyed a cold drink, while their kids played in the yard or in a nearby vacant lot. Yet, today it is quite different. Now, unfortunately people tend to spend so much more of their time indoors with their air conditioners running, never catching a glimpse of their neighbors. I believe televisions and computers have also contributed to this change. Each of these new inventions has given us more reasons to stay inside, away from the fresh air, the light of day and the other folks who live close by.

Almost every waking hour of my childhood was spent outside, playing with the other kids in the neighborhood. In the summertime we kept ourselves out of trouble by staying busy, playing a wide variety of games from early morning and on through the day. We played until we were called to come home to wash up for dinner. On many of those warm evenings, we would resume our activities after dinner and continue to play until after dark by shifting our play area to a spot under a corner streetlight. We played almost every outdoor game you can imagine. We shot marbles and spun tops. We played games of kick-the-can, hide n' seek, king-sticks and hound n' the hare. If enough boys could scrounge up roller-skates, we sometimes had a fierce game of street hockey.

With each passing year, our interest in playing the major sports increased until we reached a point where we would dedicate almost all of our outdoor time to games of baseball, football and basketball. The biggest obstacle we had when it came to playing these sports was the lack of equipment. But we were more than just competitive, we were also a very resourceful bunch. There were times when we used old cloth bags or pieces of wood for bases, and we often repaired our broken bats with nails. Sometimes we hung around outside of Bain Field during a game or during batting practice, hoping to snag a foul ball and run off with it undetected. If we could get our hands on one of those official pro baseballs, we would use it until we literally knocked its cover off. At that time we would convince our friend, the guy who worked down at the neighborhood gas station to cover and recover our treasure with black friction tape, as often as was necessary to make the baseball last for an entire summer.

Yet, we made out fine, putting everything we had to good use. All of us had a patch or two on our pants and maybe a few mended tears on our shirts but we were bathed and clean before bedtime, ready for the next active day that lay ahead. There was one thing I guess that could be said about all of us, we were poor, but didn't know it!

Today, I am amazed when I reminisce about our old neighborhood gang and count the success stories that first took root in the Park Place section of Norfolk. I spent countless days outside in the sun with young boys like Don Howren and Pete Easterling. Don's father was the owner of the Norfolk Shamrocks, a minor league football team affiliated with the Washington Redskins. Whenever our gang gathered for a pickup game of football, we could always count on Don to furnish a top-of-the-line football. It was Pete's dad who worked for the railroad and not only made enough money to own a car, but could also afford to buy gasoline. There was also Buddy Griffin and another fellow named Hobbs Howell, who was the oldest of our bunch. I was with Hobbs at the train station the day he left home to report for combat duty with our armed forces in the South Pacific. I was with Hobbs again to meet his train, the day he returned home from overseas. I guess I had matured a little while he was away, as he didn't recognize me at first. And he too looked a little different, with his skin yellowed from the Atabrine he had been given to ward off malaria. Also, there were Bobby Doumar and William McIntosh, who were both longtime members of our play gang.

Each of these fellows moved on to become prominent figures in his chosen profession and each has worked dutifully to make this world a better place. Don graduated from the William and Mary School of Law and eventually became Commonwealth's Attorney and judge for Henrico County, Virginia. Pete had a very distinguished military career and is now officially referred to as Admiral Crawford Easterling, USN, Ret. Bobby Doumar graduated from the University of Virginia with a law degree and is currently a retired U.S. Federal Judge. William founded the famous Norfolk-based photography studio, McIntosh Portraits. While he is internationally known for his photographic techniques and creativity, he has also been recognized as one of the top five photographers in the world by a leading trade magazine. It goes without saying that some very successful individuals came from our old neighborhood. Many of my old playmates grew up to assume prominent positions in life, while making positive contributions that have helped to shape the lives of others.

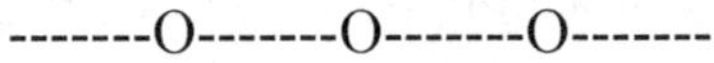

The huge brick building is still in use today. It is James Monroe Elementary School over on West 29th Street. This is where, at age six, I began my formal education and still today, for nine months out of every year the school is filled to capacity with young students from the Park Place neighborhood. Our family, like most families of the time, made a few basic considerations when planning to move to a new community. Of primary importance to most families was the close proximity of the new school and a suitable church. Grocery markets and other types of stores also had to be close by, while keeping in mind that walking would have to cover all distances around town. For me, the daily walk to Monroe Elementary was about ten city blocks, including a couple of cut-throughs, which saved me a minute or two. Back then it seemed like anything we needed and anywhere we wanted to go was always only a few blocks away from our house.

Among my fondest memories of attending Monroe Elementary was the great food we were served in the school's lunchroom. On most school days, I took a lunch that Momma had prepared for me at home. The lunches she packed were always tasty and usually included cookies to go along with a sandwich or two. But it was a special treat for me to be given lunch money to spend at the cafeteria. Momma knew how much I craved chow mein, so if I let her know in advance when it would be served, she would give me a nickel to cover the cost of my favorite lunchtime dish. That's right, five cents was all that was charged for chow mein, along with hefty portions of rice and noodles! Five cents could also get you a sandwich or a large bowl of vegetable beef soup, if you didn't bring your lunch from home.

During the warmer months of the year, I would try to make it to the school extra early in the mornings to get a place on the ball field for the morning game of *Round Tip*. This game was our informal variation of baseball, which allowed any of the kids to join in at the time they arrived at the schoolyard. If the game was already underway when a boy showed up for school, he could place his books and lunch in an area to the side of the ball diamond and take a position on the field, hoping the batter would hit the ball his way. The player who caught a pop-up or threw a runner out as he ran the bases would then get a turn to be the next hitter. The game would continue until we heard the clanging of the nine o'clock bell. That's when we all scurried to our classrooms to start another school day.

What I may have lacked in academic prowess, I made up in various extracurricular activities. It was during my later years at Monroe Elementary that I was duly appointed to be a member of the school's Safety Patrol. Wearing my white Safety Patrolman's belt across my shoulder with my shiny silver badge, I helped keep the grounds, the halls and the adjacent streets of James Monroe Elementary safe for all my fellow students. The prestige that came with this assignment made me the envy of many of the other guys around school. It was a big deal to be eleven or twelve years old and to get to tell the other kids at school what to do!

For me, self-confidence is a quality I always found to be close at hand. It was noticeable at an early age that I had no qualms about speaking with strangers or performing before an audience. One year, as the holiday season drew near, our class began to make preparations for the school's annual Christmas pageant. Before our first rehearsal, our teacher made her selections, assigning each of her pupils to play a part in the Nativity Story. Was it ironic that she chose me to play the part of one of the *Three Wise Men*? Are you kidding, me as a wise man? I was always quick to say that the role was a perfect fit for me!

Oddly enough, a few of my classmates were surprised to see my high level of interest in the school's Glee Club. Of course the club was composed of mostly girls, but I didn't mind that at all. Along with a few other brave little boys, I could be found on the back row, singing my little heart out. I was sometimes questioned by other kids in the group about what I did with the money Mom and Dad gave me to pay for singing lessons. What a senseless question to ask! It only proved that these fellows didn't know me very well. Had they really known me, there would have been no need to answer.

"I lost it all in downtown Norfolk.... at the Monroe Pool Hall!"

CHAPTER 3

LISTEN TO WHAT YOUR FATHER SAYS!

Our world was enduring some of the darkest days the human race will ever know. The forces of Nazi Germany had advanced through much of Europe with their ruthless attempt to brutally exterminate an entire race, while the Japanese were viciously executing their own brand of horror on the world. It was the early 1940s and our nation could no longer stand idly by and watch as the free world was devoured piece by piece by cruel, power-hungry dictators. The United States had no choice but to be drawn into World War II and there were few American cities that felt the effects of The War more than my hometown, Norfolk.

As one of the major centers for military operations in the country, Norfolk saw a large portion of its male population dispatched for combat duty around the world, while at home, the local factories and shipyards geared up with work shifts around the clock to meet the demands of a country at war. I was just a young fellow when I saw some of the older guys around the neighborhood leave home to serve overseas. This was as close as I would get to having my life directly affected by the war and for most of us kids in the neighborhood, life went on as usual. Of course we purchased savings stamps at school whenever we could and participated in community scrap drives, which was our way of providing extra materials for our fighting men. And as in all other American coastal cities at the time, youngsters were excited about helping grownups prepare for blackout drills. However, instead of checking the newspapers and following the progress of the war, we were focused more on other news. For instance, the news of Bob Feller of the Cleveland Indians enlisting in the U.S. Navy and reporting for duty in Norfolk or the talk around town that Gary Cooper was starring in the role of Lou Gehrig in the hit film *Pride of the Yankees,* which was coming soon to the local movie house, managed to grab our attention. But who could blame us? We were young and carefree and had our entire lives stretched out before us.

As far back as I can remember, I was always competitive, regardless of my age and no matter the sport. I wanted nothing more than to excel as an individual and be a part of the winning team. Yet in spite of my love for football and basketball, baseball was always my true passion, and so it was with my father. No doubt, it was his influence and encouragement that helped to point me in that direction, but I truly believe I would have somehow been drawn to baseball sooner or later on my own. My dad raised me to play baseball and there were occasions when he insisted that I not participate in certain scholastic activities, such as wrestling or playing football my senior year, for fear of injuries that could jeopardize my chances for a future in baseball. It was my dad that emphatically ordered me never to be a catcher for that very reason. But me, I was born with a stubborn streak a mile wide and sometimes the urge to test the waters on my own brought me a lot of pain and regret, which could have been easily averted if only I had done as I was told.

It was on a hot summer day when I was only about six or seven years old when the temptation to squat down behind home plate and catch a few pitches was too much for me to resist. Our neighborhood pick-up team needed a catcher and I was the most suitable candidate as I possessed a couple of qualities that set me apart from the other boys. First, there was my pudgy physique, which was ideal for the position. I had been convinced by the other boys that I had the perfect build for stopping wild pitches and blocking the plate if a base runner tried to score with a hard slide. Also, the possibility of getting hurt never crossed my mind; I was fearless. Because of the dangers of being hit by the bat or a foul tip, most of the other boys would never consider being a catcher, not to mention the lack of protective equipment. Whenever we gathered on the sandlot to play ball, we typically had only one bat and one ball and often no more than two or three gloves which were shared by both sides. For some crazy reason, the guys never considered catcher to be a position worthy of having the use of a glove. So when I blindly took my place behind the batter, I was completely exposed and vulnerable with no mask, no chest protector, no shin guards, nothing! Without even wearing a glove, there I was, disregarding my daddy's orders and risking life and limb for the good of the team.

We had played only a couple of innings in the scorching sun of the early afternoon when the inevitable took place. Everything was going well and my thoughts were on nothing more than winning the game, when the batter at the plate unleashed a mighty swing. His bat made only partial contact with the baseball, striking it off center, firing it straight back into the center of my unprotected face. The ball shot back at me, as if it had been shot out of a cannon, catching me squarely on my nose. The pain was unbelievable! Blood was running from my nose like a faucet and at first I couldn't do anything but let out a scream. I fell forward from my knees and while cupping both hands over my face, I cried like I had never cried before! Right away I knew I was in big trouble. As if the blood, tears and excruciating pain weren't enough to deal with, I knew for certain I would catch hell from Daddy, once he found out that I had disobeyed him.

It was tough to see my way with so many tears in my eyes, yet I had no choice but to walk back home and own up to what had happened. Lucky for me, Daddy was still at work when Momma met me in yard. She was unpinning the last few pieces of dry laundry from the clothesline and placing them in her basket when she turned to see me walking towards her.

"What in the world happened to you?" she demanded.

At first I couldn't answer. I could only stand before her and sob. By this time most of the bleeding had stopped, but the pain and burning in my face continued. It felt like my entire head was throbbing with each heartbeat. Dried blood was now caked below my nostrils and extended down to each side of my chin. Yet, as intense as the pain was, it was all secondary to my fear. The scary thought of what Daddy would do to me if he found out was, by far my biggest concern.

"What happened?" she asked again as she dropped the clothes basket to the ground. She placed her fingers below my chin and tilted my head back. She gave me a thorough examination, seeing for herself that my nose was still very bloody but not likely broken.

"The baseball hit me," I muttered, as I finally regained enough composure to sputter a few words.

"I hope you weren't catching behind the plate when this happened. Because you know what your father told you about being a catcher! He has warned you many times and he agreed that it was okay for you to play any place on the baseball field except catcher. Now, don't you remember him telling you that?" Momma continued with a full review of everything Daddy had said. "And if that is what you've been doing today over there on that ball field, then you are going to find yourself in a lot of trouble when he gets home!"

Momma took a deep sigh and slowly shook her head as she took one last look up my nostrils and pressed her finger tips gently on my touchy swollen cheeks.

"Okay, H. L., come on," she ordered. She hardly ever called me by my name and from my earliest memories

Momma always saw it best to call me only by my initials. Maybe it was easier for her, especially when she was angry.

"Let's go inside and get you cleaned up and let's get a piece of ice on your nose." She took me by the arm and led me through the back door and into the kitchen. With her voice softening just a little, she suggested that we get started.

"We don't have a lot of time," she said in a whisper as she glanced over at the old electric clock above the table. "Your father will be home shortly and it will probably be best if he doesn't find out. I don't think you're hurt too bad and I'm going to get you fixed up this once, but mark my words, this will be the last time. I hope you've learned your lesson," she cautioned. "Next time you better listen to what your father says!"

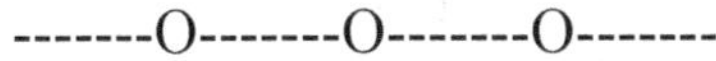

Throughout my first three years of grammar school my school work came easily. I had the luxury of maintaining grades that were well above average while expending a minimal amount of time and effort. I had been placed in advanced classes, and still my studies presented no significant challenges. I was passing all my subjects with flying colors, which meant my parents had no need to curtail my outdoor playtime for anything as distasteful as homework. But there was a change waiting for me at the midpoint of my fourth school year, one that seemed like a good idea initially, but soon proved to be a curse of sorts.

The concept of getting promoted to the next grade sounded great. Because of my impressive marks on my report cards, my parents were given an option to have me remain in the fourth grade or to forgo the second half of the grade and begin the second half of the year as a fifth grader. Mom and Dad always believed it was good for me to take advantage of all opportunities to advance and they were fully convinced that an early graduation would have its rewards for me down the road. I was excited about the possibilities and jumped at the chance to move up a grade. But I was naïve to think I could continue to cruise through my studies without taking things a little more seriously. As a fifth grader, I soon found that much of the material we covered was especially difficult for me because of some of the lessons I had skipped by bypassing a half year. After some less than satisfactory marks, it was quickly made clear to me that more time would be spent inside with my nose in my textbooks if I ever hoped to set foot on a ball field again.

Despite all that, I finished all seven grades at James Monroe Elementary over a span of six and a half years. During my last two years there, it was determined that as students, we were all mature enough to change rooms after each class, which was supposedly a way of preparing us for junior high and high school where switching rooms would be an ongoing practice. But to keep us on pace during our sixth and seventh grade years, we had music playing as we marched from one classroom to another. Old 78-RPM records of rhythmic band tunes were played on an old fashioned windup Victrola as we made our way through the halls. It was puzzling to be told that we were responsible young adults who were grown up enough to arrive at our next class on time. On the other hand, we were given only the time of one marching song to make it to the next room and to be seated in our desk, ready for class. I thought the whole procedure was like a high stakes game of musical chairs, which resulted in a tardy slip for any student who wasn't in his seat when the record ended. Oh well, there's only so much that can be said for being grown up and responsible.

I had just turned thirteen and was attending James Blair Junior High School when opportunity came a-knockin' on our family's door once again. My parents seized the chance to purchase a brand new house which was quite a bit nicer than the one we had called home for almost nine years. To me, the youngest member of the family, it seemed that we had settled perfectly into our comfortable apartment on West 27th Street and were set to stay forever. The idea of moving across town was about as far away from my mind as moving to China. So it was a memorable evening that my Daddy walked through the door and announced that he and Momma had purchased a house in Winona, another Norfolk community located a couple of miles away to the east.

Our new place at 1419 Morris Crescent, as well as the rest of our new neighborhood, took some getting used to. Yes, it was only a couple of miles from our old house, but the environment was completely different. There were new street names to learn along with new neighbors and new places to roam and play. Fortunately, I encountered some of my friends from school, since many of the kids in Winona also attended Blair Junior High.

It was about this time that I first heard the name Paul Decker. This name is one that would remain with me throughout my life. His name is one that I will always recall with respect and gratitude. It is because of this man's undying devotion to providing organized athletics for the young people of our city that many people today are able to enjoy a wide array of activities at the Norfolk Community Center, which he practically organized single-handedly.

Paul was a man of vision who would see projects through to completion. He was a sports-minded individual who had a special place in his heart for any young boy who wanted to participate in athletics and possessed an earnest desire to compete. I heard people say he was a former professional baseball player himself, who after his hopes of becoming a big leaguer were dashed, maintained connections with the Boston Red Sox, working as a bird dog scout. But he also dedicated endless hours of his time organizing sports teams for boys of all ages, making schedules and developing leagues in the three major sports. It was a plan of his to keep youngsters active and occupied, and his plan worked remarkably well. He implemented athletics as a way to keep kids off the streets and out of trouble. It was through his hard work that the Norfolk Community Leagues were organized and the Norfolk Community Center was eventually established. For several generations now, young people all over Norfolk have enjoyed athletic and recreational activities offered by the Center's branches located throughout the city. The value of his work to the city will never be fully calculated.

From the very start, the Community Leagues grabbed the attention of boys from all parts of Norfolk. From the younger fellows still in grammar school who participated in the "midget" leagues to the older guys in high school who played in the "high" leagues, organized sports were made available for all ages. Interest was high at all levels, but for those of us too young to participate in high school varsity sports, these programs gave us a great start in organized athletics and a tremendous advantage for future competition. We had teams for baseball, basketball and football, which kept us involved year round. When the season of one sport ended, it was time for another to begin, allowing very little time for any of us aspiring young athletes to find mischief.

There was no comparison between the uniforms and equipment we had for our Community League games and the colorful, matching uniforms and the expensive gear that is furnished for play in today's youth athletic programs. Even the playing fields for today's activities are professionally cut, manicured and marked off to regulation size before they kids are allowed to take the field. Yet, I dare say that anyone today can find an assortment of young boys that can match the talent, the fiery spirit or the desire to win of the fellows I played with and against all those many years ago.

Award Certificate

This is to Certify

That H.L.Foiles,Jr.

has been awarded the championship (LETTER) in football (SPORT)

for the 1943 season

Park Place,Community Junior High Football League

Coach Director

It was Paul Decker who worked hard to provide organized athletics for boys of all ages in Norfolk. At fourteen years old, I was on the Community League's football champions in the Junior High Division.

Personally, one of my proudest moments as a youngster occurred when, at twelve years old, I was awarded a small brass medal for playing for the Community League baseball champions of the midget division. It was nothing more than just a simple engraved shield with the words "Midget Yankees-1941 Community League Champions." However, because of my strong sentimental attachment to that, my first award of any kind, I may have had good reason to be upset, when I learned that the Virginia Sports Hall of Fame had "misplaced" the keepsake, along with some other personal items, which were loaned to their museum for display.

Midget Champions and Runners-Up in Junior Division

The Yankees, midget champions of the Community League. . . . Left to right, front, Crowder, Toffton, Gaskins, Lake, Acey; middle, Polizos, Copeland, Foiles, Howzen, Bill Stevens; back, Coach Black, Allison, Bobby Stevens, Ballance.

The Yankees, 1941 Midget Champions of the Community League--that's me at twelve years old, middle row, center, when I received my first award.

Conditions were much simpler for our games back then and so were so many other things in life. For example, for our Community League baseball games, we had no uniforms at all; we played in our T-shirts and jeans. For basketball, we slipped unmarked jerseys over our T-shirts. Those stinky tops were in two different colors and only worn to help tell the opposing squads apart. Prior to that, our only means for separating the teams had been to play games of "shirts" versus "skins," the most basic way of being in uniform. But, getting outfitted for our football game is another whole story in itself.

For days of practice or games, it was best if you showed up at the grammar school down at Madison Ward as early as possible to grab yourself some of the better equipment. Getting there early also helped improve your chances of finding a few items that were somewhere close to your size. We would tear through piles and piles of helmets, shoulder pads, hip pads, cleats, pants and jerseys to get the choice pickings of the lot. All the while, we considered ourselves fortunate if we found some pads, or maybe a shirt that had had a chance to partially dry out from the last game and hopefully didn't stink to high heaven! This equipment was continually used by different boys day after day and was always put away damp and allowed to "cure" overnight, acquiring an aroma that would cause a skunk to hold his nose! Once we put on our game faces and were suited up in our moldy uniforms and pads, we had to walk from the school, down Hampton Boulevard and over to the Lambert's Point section of town to our game site at Dunn Field, a hike of more than a mile. After four quarters of play on a rock-hard dusty football field, we hobbled another mile back to the school, limping all the way with our usual assortment of cuts, sprains and bruises, only to arrive covered in dirt and soaked in perspiration and so exhausted we could hardly strip off the wet, foul-smelling gear. We peeled out of our armor, piece by piece, like a bunch of butterflies wiggling from their cocoons. The gear was then tossed back into the separate piles, to be ready again for the next lucky guy who got to use it the next day.

The intersection of Eighteenth and Granby Streets was another location in Norfolk that was an additional center of activity for many of the neighborhood boys. Just a short walk from my house, that corner spot, which fronted Granby, was the site of the Dix-Bowers Tire Company, one of the more well known distributors of automobile tires on the East

Coast, a true landmark business in the community. However, it wasn't their quality tires at affordable prices that kept me going back there day after day, after school and on Saturdays. Rather, it was the second floor basketball court in that spacious old warehouse that was the site of some of the most hotly contested basketball games ever played in the city. It was the second level of that business complex that was known as the Dix-Bowers Gymnasium. The full size basketball court located upstairs above the tire business was often used for adult league play and occasionally for area semi-pro teams. But for young boys like me who lived in Park Place or one of the other surrounding neighborhoods, it was a place to spend countless hours playing games against rival neighborhood teams or competing individually in foul shot contests.

All basketball activities at the Dix-Bowers Gym were supervised by an older gentleman, known around town as Paddy Doran. Paddy, an affable bachelor who worked for the Norfolk and Western Railroad, was there every day, on schedule, opening and securing the second floor and keeping the facility ready for play. He was both our referee and coach and was always quick to offer a pointer or two to help a boy sharpen his game. He was also there to pass out towels and collect nickels as we walked up the stairs and passed through the door. That's right, nickels! Five cents was the standard fee charged to each boy who wanted to play, but back during those times a kid sure got a lot for his money. The charge included soap, a clean towel and a hot shower. Plus, as an added bonus after the game, the player who hit the most free throws out of ten chances from the foul line would have his nickel returned as his prize. For us a nickel was a swell prize for the winner and certainly no small amount to sneeze at. It was just enough to entice each of us to painstakingly shoot our best two-handed, underhanded shots while under the pressure of having all the other boys watching and jeering during the entire contest. After each shootout there was never any doubt about what the winning player would do with his prize money, as we were all aware that our favorite treat was waiting, just down the street and around the corner at Birtcherd's Dairy Store.

Birtcherd's, a popular ice cream spot, was the favorite of kids and grownups from all around town. There, it was two-scoops for just five cents, with just about any flavor of ice cream you could imagine to choose from. Now, with a frozen treat like that available for just five cents, it's easy to see why every kid in the league tried so hard to be the free-throw champion!

And while we are on the subject of tasty sweets, there was another source in town for a sugary favorite that was available to only a select few of us kids. The place to go was Doumar's Barbeque down on Monticello Avenue at 20th Street, and to get in on the deal, you had to be friends with Bobby Doumar. Bobby, as I mentioned earlier, was one of our play gang in the Park Place neighborhood and it was our good fortune that his father and uncle just happened to own the place. Doumar's served up a lot more than barbeque sandwiches, French fries and sodas. They also stacked up some of the best ice cream cones in town. While none of us boys ever had two pennies to rub together, we had Bobby as a friend, whom we could always count on to make a hike down to 20th Street worth our time. We seldom had the luxury of enjoying the great ice cream, but we sure had lots of chances to sample leftovers from the cone-making operation.

Bobby would have us stay out on the sidewalk just outside the front door, while he entered the shop and headed straight for the kitchen area. In just a few minutes he would return carrying a paper bag filled with pieces of the sugar cones. These were golden brown chunks of broken cones that were his for the taking. Made almost entirely from sugar, and one or two secret ingredients for extra flavor, those broken shards made the best snack whenever we took a timeout from our carefree day of romping and playing around the neighborhood. It wasn't that we needed the extra energy from all that sugar, it was the delicious taste and the fact that it was free, that kept us coming back again and again. It was his Uncle Abe who allowed Bobby to go in and gather up the fragments of broken cones. However, it is interesting to note that it was his Grandfather Abe Doumar, a Syrian immigrant, who made a landmark discovery in the confectionary industry when he invented the first ice cream cone. He sold his new idea from a vendor's stand at the St. Louis Exposition in 1904. There may still be some other stories that circulate about the making of the first cone, but none that are documented as thoroughly as the historical account of Bobby's Uncle Abe. As the story goes, Abe Doumar ran out of the small cups he used for serving ice cream and was forced to improvise in order to keep up with sales. He began making thin crispy waffles which were rolled into round, funnel-shaped, edible holders for his frozen treats. With his quick thinking and resourcefulness, the first ice cream cone was invented. Now, more than a century later, some of his original waffle- making machinery is still in service at Doumar's Barbeque Stand in Norfolk, while more of it is on permanent display in The Smithsonian Institution in Washington D.C.

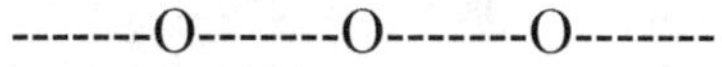

I had no way to foresee how playing in a local basketball league with my friends from around town would lead to a life changing encounter, a meeting with a gentleman which would impact my future not only as an athlete, but also as a person. As a believer that all things happen for a reason, I can now see that it was my association with Paddy Doran that made it possible for me to meet the man who, with the exception of my father, would have more influence on me than any other man in my life.

Paddy Doran was friend to all of us boys who played ball there at the Dix-Bowers Gym. He was an unassuming, likeable fellow who knew all of us by name and was familiar with our family situations as well. He would never hesitate to give any of us a ride home if our game ran a little late and we would all get a big kick out of riding in Paddy's old Ford Club Coupe, "Wintergreen." His vehicle was appropriately named by the boys at the gym because of the breathtaking piny, wintergreen odor that filled its interior. The aroma was the result of so many bottles of athletic rubbing liniment that had been spilled on the seats and floor over the years. Yet, the man and his car seemed to be such a perfect fit. When you know a fellow who dedicated himself to working with young athletes and who loved sports as much as Paddy Doran, what else could you expect?

It was Paddy Doran who set the wheels in motion for that special introduction to take place. He was the person who saw me as a young boy with athletic potential that he believed was deserving of some extra attention. I'll never know what it was that Paddy detected in me or what he noticed that was out of the ordinary. Maybe it was my attitude or perhaps my determination. But whatever it was that he detected, his confidence in me was enough to have him recommend me to one of the greatest high school coaches ever in the history of Virginia sports.

I was fourteen with almost a year left to go in junior high school when Paddy approached me at the gym. The game was over, I had showered and dressed and was heading for the door when he called me aside, wanting a quick word.

"I spoke with a friend of mine who would like to talk to you sometime soon," he said, sparking my curiosity. "He's the head coach over at the new high school, Granby High. I had a talk with him the other day and your name came up in the conversation. He seems to be interested in meeting with you. His name is Coach Bill Story," he added.

I took a quick look around to make sure there were no eavesdroppers in the area. Paddy was speaking in a soft and serious tone, a tone that would surely attract the attention of the other boys if they could have been close enough to hear.

"Sure, Paddy, I've heard of Coach Story. But what would he want to see me about?" I asked. "I still have another year to go before I attend high school."

"I know, Henry, but that year will be over before you know it. Besides, he is very determined to build a good sports program over at the new school and he will need boys who are both good students as well as good athletes to do it."

We stood quietly for just a moment as I struggled to be clear about the point Paddy was trying to make.

"But, I don't think I'll be going to the new school, Paddy. The high school students in my area will all be going to Maury High. Isn't that right?" I questioned.

"Don't be so sure about that, Henry," he warned. "Coach Story said that it may be possible that the kids in Winona where you live may have a choice to make about which school to attend. It seems that your neighborhood falls directly on the border of the two school districts, so you and your parents may have a big decision to make before school starts next year."

Naturally I had been thinking about entering high school in another year and about how great it would be to play high school football and other sports, but this talk about choosing between two schools was all new to me. This whole idea of Paddy's had caught me by surprise, but it sounded like a good one. Patty went on to explain further.

"I told Coach Story that you might be the type of boy he was looking for. I told him your grades are pretty good, you'd be willing to work hard and that you're a good athlete who will always hustle and give your best effort on the field."

This recommendation that Paddy made on my behalf was very flattering, I thought. But this whole deal would be a matter that I would need to talk over with my parents before we took it any further.

Patty gave me one last suggestion before I started down the steps. "Okay, Henry, let me ask you this. The next time you are here at the gym, what do you say if you and I hop in ol' Wintergreen and take a ride over to Granby High? We'll drop by Coach Story's office and pay him a visit. I have a feeling that it would be great to get the two of you together. It would be good for both of you."

"Okay, Patty," I responded. "Let me talk this over at home and if you're sure this is a good idea, then I'll be happy to take that ride with you."

Like I always say, everything happens for a reason.

CHAPTER 4

GLORY DAYS AT GRANBY

I wasn't sure what to expect, but Paddy had my complete trust from the very start. The two of us walked around the perimeter of the gymnasium floor and found that the door to the coach's office was left open. It was his idea to visit Coach Story, and now to notice that his door was intentionally left open suggested that he might be approachable. The decision about which high school to attend had been thoroughly discussed at home and I had reached a point with my parents where they were ready for me to make a decision and choose the school where I would be most happy. Yet, they insisted that I learn as much as I could about both of the high schools before enrolling in either.

"Take your time, son, and ask a lot of questions," Dad advised. So taking advantage of a chance to meet with Coach Bill Story was something both of my parents fully endorsed. Paddy could see that someone was in the office and stuck his head through the doorway.

"Do you have a minute, Coach?" Paddy asked, as he lightly rapped on the door frame with the back of his hand.

I stepped around Paddy to a place where I could see inside the office. There was someone seated at a desk whose face broke into a big smile when he glanced up from his work and saw who was calling on him.

"Why, Paddy, of course I do. I'll always have time for you!" the man answered.

The well-groomed gentleman pushed his chair away from his desk and rose to his feet. He quickly extended his hand to Paddy for a hearty handshake. There was no doubting the friendship between these two fellows.

"Good to see you again, Coach," Paddy said in response to the warm reception. "I hope we're not interrupting you, but I thought I would drop by for a minute and introduce you to my friend, Henry Foiles. Henry is the fellow I mentioned who may be coming here to Granby in September."

The trim, athletic looking man walked from behind the desk and invited me to step into his office.

"Come on in, Henry," he urged. "Paddy has told me a little bit about you and it's good to finally meet you. Paddy said that you have a decision to make about where to go to school this fall and he also told me that you are quite an athlete."

He then reached out to me to shake hands, a seemingly simple gesture, but one that made a lasting impression. His grip, as I well remember, was firm and his eyes peered directly into mine. Even today, I believe these mannerisms often speak volumes about a man's character. This man demonstrated a confident presence which immediately drew my attention and respect. He then took the lead in what would be the first of countless conversations between us.

"I'm happy that you fellows took time to stop by. Have a seat and let's talk for a few minutes," the coach offered.

I took a seat in a folding chair near the door and took a quick look around, noting the framed black and white photos hanging about the small room. The pictures were all of football players some accepting trophies and some posing with their coaches. I sat back in the seat and placed my hands on my thighs, trying to appear at ease and confident, only to realize that I had not uttered a single word up to this point.

"Well, Henry," Coach Story continued, "as you already know we have a new athletic program here at Granby High School and it's going to require a lot of careful planning and hard work to get started on the right foot. Now, Paddy here has told me that you're a hard worker and according to him you take your training seriously and that's required of all of the boys who play any sport for me. And frankly, Henry, we don't have a lot of time. It's almost time for football practice to begin and before you know it, classes will start." At that point the coach paused and saw that he had my full attention. "Now going by what Paddy has told me," he continued, "there is no question that I'd like to see you come to Granby and come out for football, but I want you to know ahead of time what will be expected from you and from all of the boys who come out. Now I'm expecting to have some good players on my squad this season and you can be one of them, Henry, if you're willing to keep working hard all through the season. I'd like to see you earn a starting spot on this team, but it certainly won't be handed to you. You'll earn it if you get it and it won't be an easy job!"

There was a moment of stillness as Coach Story paused again. He looked over at Paddy to see if he had earned approval on his approach and philosophy. Paddy slowly nodded in agreement, but didn't say a word. Coach then turned to me, checking for a reaction. He was looking to determine if I was discouraged or intimidated by his adamant demands, or to see if I was charged-up and motivated by his serious, no-nonsense approach to his job and to the game of football.

"Don't get me wrong, Henry," he continued, "we'll have a lot of fun. I think you'll like playing for me and you'll enjoy it here at Granby, but the hard work will come first, both in the classroom and on the football field. Afterward, when the long, hot practice sessions with the blocking, the hitting and the wind sprints are over, that's when we'll have fun. That's when we will reap our rewards. We'll have fun when we are successful on the field on game day!"

I was completely overwhelmed and thoroughly impressed by what this man had just laid out before me. His requirements were precisely what I had imagined the ideal football coach would demand of his players. It was nothing more than what I would require of myself and of any of my teammates, that is to work hard and always give it his best. I knew right away that I not only wanted to play football for this man, but I wanted to get to know him better.

Paddy Doran had always spoken very highly of Coach Story and now I had seen for myself the reason why. The coach's demeanor, his integrity and sincere dedication to his work all made a deep impression on me there in that tiny office. With this our first meeting, and even at my young age I knew I wanted to follow him. The impact of meeting him had me anxious to go to battle with him and give him my best efforts.

At this stage of our meeting I knew it was time for me to respond and express myself in some way. I needed to speak up and take part in the conversation and show my interest. While at the same time, I needed to curb my enthusiasm. I came very close to announcing right then that I would enroll at Granby for the next school year and that I was ready to sign up for his football team right there on the spot. But I managed to contain myself as I didn't want to come across as being overly anxious and immature. I needed to be thoughtful and speak sensibly, knowing that there is only one chance to make a first impression.

"That all sounds great to me, Coach," I sputtered. "You've given me a lot to think about and I appreciate you taking time to talk with me. I think I'd like to play for Granby this season, but I'll have to talk it over with Mom and Dad when I get home and then I'll let you know as soon as I can."

"That'll be fine, Henry," the coach assured me. "I'm sure you and your parents will arrive at the right decision and please let them know that I'll be happy to meet with them at anytime, if they have any questions. Just have them give me a call."

I didn't even notice the odor of liniment as Paddy drove me home in ol' Wintergreen. I had much, too much, on my mind to let the smell bother me. Neither of us had much to say while he drove through the heavy evening traffic. But I had a strong hunch that Paddy could tell that my mind was already made up. He was reading me like a book.

Maury High School, the older established school had served all of the high school students from the Winona area up until this time. However, due to a questionable order from the school board, any student from that neighborhood who chose to attend the new high school, Granby, was required to go through the normal registration and begin the new school year at Maury, however, after attending the first day of classes at Maury, the student was then eligible to transfer. For a time I felt much like a show dog, being forced to jump through hoops for no good, understandable reason. Yet, I went along with the whole crazy process and became a freshman at Granby High School on the second day of the school year. I convinced myself that it was a simple formality that I could live with, since it meant that I would be with Coach Story from then on.

My association with Coach Bill Story was no short-lived connection. As time passed, it evolved into the type of relationship that happens only once in a lifetime. Over the years it became a close enduring friendship that was founded on mutual respect, admiration and trust. He was a remarkable man with strong convictions and a philosophy about competition and about life which proved to be very beneficial to many young men who came under his tutelage. I can't recall any boy he taught or coached that ever went bad. While not every one of them made it to the top of his profession, I know of none who failed in life.

William J. Story Jr. went on to become head football coach at Davidson College in North Carolina. Years later, in what would be a completely different capacity, he used his outstanding leadership skills to serve as the Superintendent of Schools for the South Norfolk Public School System. Eventually, as his focus turned to politics, he became active in matters regarding the integration of Norfolk's public schools and he was named to the Virginia State Board of Education. The culmination of his political interests came in 1965 when he represented the Virginia Conservative Party in that year's race for governor. While Mills Godwin Jr. took the election as the Democratic Party candidate, Coach Story made quite a showing for himself and his platform by securing thirteen percent of the total vote. His integrity and sensible approach to social and political issues caught the attention of many Virginians that year.

Looking back, it is easy to see that my entire life took off in a new direction after just one encounter with Coach Bill Story. With the exception of my father, no other man had as much influence on the course of my life as he did. We remained close over the years, through my time in major league baseball and also through the years that followed. I often sensed that Coach Story was proud of me, not just for my athletic accomplishments, but also for my hard work and the dedication which were vital to my success. No doubt, he was very instrumental in laying the groundwork for my long career in sports, yet I will always feel endeared to him as a person of like convictions.

With the exception of my father, no man had more influence on the course of my life than William J. Story Jr.

I was never more honored than when this long-time mentor of mine asked that I be the one individual to introduce him at a political campaign gathering at the Monticello Hotel in Norfolk on the evening he accepted his party's nomination for Virginia's gubernatorial race. I was so honored by his request that at once I began to jot down notes, creating an outline of my thoughts, which I thought would help me through a few difficult minutes of public address. However, just moments before I stepped to the podium to speak, I threw my index cards aside and decided to speak in an unrehearsed, off the cuff manner. My introduction went surprisingly well. It may have been a little lengthy, yet I had so much to say about this man, I wholeheartedly supported. That evening I spoke to the audience with heartfelt convictions which were enough to take me through the introduction without any hesitation and without once stumbling on my words.

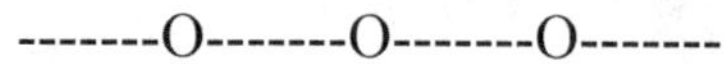

Over time, my choice to enroll at Granby High School proved to be the right one. It wasn't long before I could see how, on a personal level, it was one of the more positive and beneficial decisions I would make in life. During my high school years, I was led to another individual who would further impact my life in a very unusual and unexpected way. My first encounter with this person came when, with the exception of track, I was participating in just about all team sports at the school. Little did I know that I would soon be adding that sport to my list of athletic activities.

There were perhaps six, maybe eight, of us, bare-footed boys milling about the edge of the gymnasium floor, waiting for the start of our morning physical education class, when I suddenly became distracted. I found that my attention had been redirected away from the other boys and our idle horseplay to a set of three wooden javelins which were hanging on the wall just inside the coach's office. I'm sure they were there long before that day, but for some strange reason they grabbed my attention and like a moth drawn to a flame, I began to saunter towards the office, edging a little closer to them with each step. But unlike that moth, I should have known that nothing any good would ever come from playing with fire. My curiosity was getting the better of me. As I got closer, I could see that the javelins were rough and warped, not in the best condition. But this did nothing to curb my curiosity. Taking a look around, I quickly surveyed the situation and concluded that no one of authority was watching and that I should go ahead, satisfy my fascination with this equipment and try one of them out for myself. They were just begging to be thrown and I couldn't resist!

With all the nervousness of a rookie cat burglar on his first heist, I lifted one of the spears from its mounts and began to tiptoe in the direction of the gym's back door. As if tip-toeing would help me get outside undetected, I stepped softly until I made it outdoors, behind the gym to the football practice field. Once there, I began to amuse myself. I made several tosses and found myself adding distance with each try. Still, I had no idea if I was getting off any good throws or not, because my complete ignorance of javelin competition had me clueless about what I was doing. I was having the time of my life as I launched one last throw, high, straight and long. Oddly, this time it didn't sound just right when hit the ground. This one didn't land like the others. This time it sounded more like a crash, like wood cracking and splitting as it struck the hard bare dirt of the practice field. As I slowly drew closer, I could easily see a large ragged crack in the spear, running lengthwise just below the tip and extending back several inches. The split in the wooden shaft was much too big for me to consider hiding, so I immediately began to feel a burning lump starting to form in my throat. I knew I was in big trouble. I had passed the point of no return!

My best chance of getting out of this jam, I reasoned, *would be to return this broken javelin back to its original place and hope like the Dickens that there was still no one around to see what I was up to, just as it was when I first came up with this sneaky idea.* I soon discovered that I was in this mess all alone. Even my old friend Lady Luck had abandoned me.

Inside the gymnasium, I tentatively made my way toward the coach's office, still toting the destroyed javelin. When I was about to step foot into the office, the door to the tiny men's room located only a few feet away popped open. Suddenly, startling me and causing me to practically jump to the ceiling was the school's varsity track coach, Coach Ray Casey!

"What in the world do you think you're doing, Foiles?" he bellowed as he stomped towards me. "You're not a member of the track team and you have no business handling that equipment. So let's get something straight, right now! As long as I am the track coach here at Granby, you are not to touch any of this equipment that belongs to my track team! Do we understand each another?"

Coach Casey's tirade had been loud enough to reach even the most distant corners of the school. Hoping that it was over, I was shaking my head in agreement long before I could respond.

Having been caught red-handed, there was little I could do. "Yes sir, Coach Casey, I fully understand!" were about the only words I could muster at the time. I was grasping for straws, but I knew there was nothing I could do to wiggle off the hook. My situation was hopeless, so I decided to fess-up and face the music.

"But look, Coach," I interjected, "this javelin has a crack in it!"

He spun back around abruptly to face me. "A what?" he asked.

"A crack, it's broken. I didn't do it intentionally, but I broke it when I took it outside," I offered.

"Well that's just fine!" he shot back. "That's exactly what happens when you use things that you know nothing about! You had no business going into my office and taking something that isn't yours and none of your concern. Don't ever touch any of these javelins again!"

True, it wasn't any of my concern at the time, and it wouldn't be… until later in the school year.

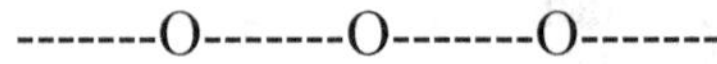

It looked like winter was finally giving up for another year and making way for springtime, the time for warmer weather and for playing baseball. It was that wonderful time of year, when after-school baseball practice sessions were well underway and the smell of freshly cut grass filled the chilly air. It was the early part of the season when the baseball continued to sting a little through my mitt because of the lingering cool temperatures.

Our squad was on the ball diamond finishing up what had been a rigorous preseason workout while a few of us had paired up and were lobbing baseballs back and forth. Some of the fellows were talking it up, probably voicing their opinions about the biggest sports debate of the time: Who's the better all-around player, Joe DiMaggio or Ted Williams?

All the while I was noticing that the school's track team was warming up in an area near the baseball field. For those fellows it was a big day. It was time for the all important qualifying trials. No doubt, many of them were feeling the pressure and carried high hopes of qualifying for the team's first track meeting of the season which was only about two weeks away. By this time the baseball team had ended their day, I found myself to be the only player left on the diamond as the track team started their first event. I had no reason to hurry home except to get started on my homework, so I decided to stay back for a few moments and watch the track trials, particularly my favorite, the javelin event.

Once the baseball field had been deserted, the track team began to migrate over into the outfield area. I stood along the right field line and watched as the first throws of the javelin competition got underway. The spears began to sail in my direction. First one and then another landed on the grass not far from me. After the first set of throws, I thought I would be helpful and throw the javelins back towards the left field area, so the competitors would not have to retrieve them. I grasped one at mid-length with my right hand and held it horizontally about shoulder high. With a running start, I made a couple of strides forward and released it, sending the pole hurtling through the air, back to the area from where it came. I picked up another and again, I used my untrained form to launch it back towards the track team. Not knowing if anyone else was noticing, it became obvious to me that my tosses were considerably longer than any of the throws made so far in the trials. Suddenly I began to have thoughts about the last time I threw a javelin and recalled the firestorm that erupted when Coach Casey caught me trying to sneak a broken one back to his office. Those thoughts were enough to make me decide I had better be on my way home. I was intrigued by the trials and would have liked to stick around to watch, but I wanted no more trouble with Coach Casey. He had made it clear months earlier that I was not to touch any of his track team's equipment, so I decided I would avoid any possible trouble and make my way over to the gym to pick up my books.

Before I could make more than a step or two, the manager of the track team came dashing across the outfield grass, heading towards me and yelling to me.

"Hey, Foiles!" he yelled from just outside of the foul line. "Coach Casey wants to see you! He wants to talk to you right away!

"Oh boy," I mumbled under my breath. "He's really going to let me have it this time for messing with his equipment again," I convinced myself.

I jammed my baseball mitt under my arm and took off across the ball field. I had no trouble spotting Coach Casey as he stood surrounded by a mob of hopeful athletes. He stared intently at his clipboard as he seemed to tune out the chatter going on around him. As I stepped closer to him, he grabbed the whistle which dangled from a string around his neck and placed it between his teeth. He took a deep breath and was about to give it a blast when I cleared my throat to let him know I was there.

"I'm sorry, Coach. I'll never pick up another one of those things, ever again," I promised, admitting my guilt. "I just thought I'd give your boys a hand so they wouldn't have to walk so far to get them back."

"Never mind that, Foiles," he snapped. No doubt, he wanted to change the subject and move away from my past offenses. "I want to see you throw those javelins again, but this time from the scratch line."

"I'm sorry Coach, I don't understand. What's a scratch line?" I asked. He had me totally confused. I had no clue of what he was talking about and no idea of what he had in mind. I'm sure the other boys were confused as well, seeing how the qualifying trials were being interrupted by our conversation

I followed behind him for a few steps until he stopped and picked up a javelin from the ground. He placed it in my hands and began to give me a few basic instructions.

"I want you to show me some good throws, similar to the ones you made a while ago from over near first base. Now, move back a few paces behind this scratch line and build up some steam before you let it go. Just be sure to release it before you cross that line."

He watched me closely as I got off about three or four throws. He nodded his head in approval and ordered me to continue with a couple more. Finally, he had seen enough.

"Okay, Henry, that's all. Good job. You are now a member of the track team!" he announced. "Come see me tomorrow about this same time and we'll get you started."

I'm sure my mouth dropped open in disbelief. Maybe I did hear him correctly.

"Oh no, Coach," I tried to explain. "You don't understand. I'm on the baseball team and I won't have time to be on the track team too."

Granby High's track coach, Ray Casey, considered me to be his personal "diamond in the rough."

"Sure you can, Henry," he countered. "You don't have baseball on Saturdays and that's the day we have our track meets. I'll set aside extra time to work with you on the javelin throw and you'll pick it up in no time. You'll have enough time to do that along with baseball and I'm sure you'll do well in both sports."

It only took about two weeks of working with Coach Casey for me to learn that he was a man of vision. He quickly instilled confidence in me and earned my respect. He taught me a lot about the proper techniques of javelin competition and helped refine my form. Since all of this was happening during my junior year at Granby High, it was only natural that there were a few dissenters around school who felt that it was too late for me to take up a new sport, while others claimed I had no business trying to play two sports at the same time. Yet, Coach Casey saw things from a different perspective. He considered me to be his personal "diamond in the rough." Not only was I successful in my first competitive meet with a toss of 142 feet, but I continued to win all of my events as we wound our way through the team's schedule of 1946. At the conclusion of the track season, in an Eastern Virginia regional meet, I managed a throw of 196 feet, 7 inches, which was a record-setting distance for the state of Virginia in high school javelin competition. It was by far the best distance of any of the other competitors for that event. But this is where an ironic twist comes into the story.

Soon after the final scheduled meet of the season, I was surprised when I received some very flattering news. I was shocked to learn that I had received an invitation to participate in the famous Penn Relays which are held annually at the University of Pennsylvania's Franklin Field. I was humbled by the recognition associated with this invitation and for the days that followed, the excitement and attention had my head in the clouds. It was a tremendous honor that I hadn't anticipated; however, I was suddenly faced with making a difficult choice.

As fate would have it, there was also a regional high school track meet slated for the same day as the Penn Relays. After struggling for several days to reach a decision, I declined the invitation to Philadelphia for the prestigious event, so I could join my team-mates from Granby for that day, instead of competing for myself as an individual in another state. I was forced to balance the pros and cons of the situation and I am proud to say that my decision came down on the side of loyalty. I felt like I owed it to Coach

Casey and to my fellow Comets to be with them whenever we faced the other area high schools. However, I was quite unnerved when the final results of the meet in Philadelphia reached home.

Each year the Penn Relays draw thousands of the best athletes from all over North America and abroad. Therefore, any sanctioned marks set in that competition are recorded and recognized as international records. If my memory serves me correctly, the javelin competition at the Penn Relays that day was won by a young cadet from the U.S. Naval Academy named Herschel Held. His winning throw that day was measured at 185 feet. It occurred the same day, on which I recorded my toss of 196 feet, 7 inches! Oh well, I couldn't be at two places at the same time.

The lingering notion of knowing that my recorded distance that day at the high school regional meet would have been more than enough to garner a championship with international significance haunted me for the remainder of the track season. I was satisfied that I had done what was best for my school and for Coach Casey, yet nagging thoughts of "what if" and "if only" wanted to invade my thinking. But because I was never contrite by nature or one who wasted much time with regret, I made a concentrated effort to look to the future and soon I convinced myself that there would be other track events to help me gain recognition and other opportunities for me to prove myself in the near future.

Sure enough, after the conclusion of the season, I was notified that I had been named to *Look* magazine's All-American High School Track Team. My selection to the magazine's prestigious roster was not only a coveted accolade for young track athletes across the country, the notification arrived at the best of times for me personally. While the selection didn't cause me to lose any misgivings I had about missing the Penn Relays, it made the whole situation a lot easier to accept.

FOILES

Javelin Throw

Henry Foiles, of Granby High, Norfolk, Va., never went out for track until this year, yet tossed the javelin 196'7" in a district meet and later set a new State Meet mark of 181'11" despite a twice-injured ankle. Foiles, a Junior, is 17, 6 feet, and weighs 176 pounds.

Being selected to Look magazine's All-American High School Track Team made missing the Penn Relays a lot easier to accept.

For my final competition of the year, I went along with a few other selected members of our team from Granby High School to the campus of the University of North Carolina in Chapel Hill. We were chosen by Coach Ray Casey to participate in an invitational meet which featured both high school as well as collegiate teams. Naturally, I would be competing in my specialty event, the javelin throw, but also for this meet I would be running a 440 yard leg in the mile relay.

Upon our arrival the Tar Heel hosts really rolled out the red carpet for all of the visiting teams. The accommodations, the facilities and the food were all excellent. In addition, we quickly learned that a big school like UNC did everything in first-class fashion. They even owned some of the best athletic equipment that money could buy.

The schedule of competition for the day was arranged so that the track team of UNC as well as all of the other participating college teams, ran their events first. The high school level of competition, in which we competed, followed at a later time. The free time we had before our events allowed us to spend some time watching the collegiate action and gave us high-schoolers an opportunity to chat with a few of the older competitors. The time also allowed us to see some of the high-grade track equipment used by the older boys, especially the javelins. These javelins were like none I had ever seen before! They were some fine pieces of woodwork. Each of them was sleek and smooth, covered with multiple coats of lacquer. They were well-crafted with layered construction, through a special process of Swedish lamination and balanced to precision. You could rest any one of these spears, with its cord-wound grip area on your index finger and it would stay perfectly horizontal forever, due to its precisely engineered balance.

One of the friendly, accommodating college boys handed me one of those beautiful spears just to let me get the feel of its fine quality and craftsmanship. He pointed out some of its features and explained how the piece was far superior to any he had ever used. He even went so far as to suggest that I give it a try. He thought it might be beneficial for me, as a younger athlete, to experience the handling of such an exceptional javelin.

I took him up on his offer and decided to take this missile for a test flight. I launched it from the scratch line and let it fly into the clear North Carolina air. What a beautiful flight it made! It traveled straight and true. There was no wobbling with this staff, as it was perfectly aligned and straight, unlike the warped antique relics to which I was accustomed. It traveled high towards the sky with only a slight, yet near perfect rotation. The distance of this throw was considerably farther than even I was expecting. My immediate thoughts were all about how great it felt to use such nice equipment and how much I needed a few of these incredibly beautiful poles for myself and my teammates.

Throughout the early competition the college boys, who were there representing eight colleges and universities from the mid-Atlantic area, made countless throws with their javelins. There were so many competitors from so many schools, yet each team seemed to have brought along its own field assistants who were responsible for retrieving the spears at the end of each round. They were also to secure all other equipment at the end of the meet. However, once the javelin events for the college division were completed, those individuals were negligent and failed to do their job. All of the college teams had left the area and took off for the locker room, leaving the high-priced gear behind. Those neglected javelins gave me all the inclination I would need to take matters into my own hands.

I made a quick survey of the landscape and took note of some small hills covered with trees which stood only about one hundred fifty feet from where the forgotten javelins were left.

One hundred fifty feet, I surmised, *not too far away. For me, that's about the ideal distance.*

It seemed like such a shame that these prominent, well-to-do colleges had such nice equipment, especially those beautiful javelins, while we had none.

"They will never be missed," I told myself.

With a complete disregard for either honesty or reasoning, I snatched up eight javelins, one belonging to each of the college teams and proceeded to prove to my own satisfaction that each of them performed beautifully as I threw them one by one into the grove of trees on the near by hills.

Later, with the activities of the day finished, and the other team buses packed and on their way home, I knew it was time for me to return to the hills for a final look, to see if I could still locate the forgotten javelins. I felt duty-bound as an athlete and an individual who appreciated high quality sporting goods, to retrieve those javelins and not permit such nice equipment to lie on the grass where they may soon be damaged by the damp night air. So, later that evening all eight of those valuable spears found their way back to Norfolk, Virginia. Needless to say, they were stored away quietly and somehow became part of our athletic arsenal at Granby High.

At the time, we all had high hopes for the next upcoming season of track and field for the Comets and no one was more positive than I was. I was already anticipating a great senior year, hoping to repeat as a state champion in my specialized event. But, you know what they say, "What goes around, comes around."

I never got an opportunity to put those wonderful Swedish laminated javelins to good use and I never came close to another shot at improving my state record. Due to some questionable safety concerns, the Virginia High School League decided to drop the javelin throw competition from its track and field events before the start of the following school year. But maybe it was all for the best. It was starting to seem like javelins, no matter who they belonged to, never brought me anything but trouble!

Dear Henry:

It is with a great deal of regret that I leave Granby High School. All the students of this school, from the lowest to the highest, have cooperated to the "nth" degree and made my life here extremely pleasant.

I am particularly sorry to leave the members of the 1945 football team. You were a great organization with all the poise and confidence that makes for success. I trust that you will never forget, however, that you should always be a man first and a football player second. Your ability to play football, instead of giving you the right to trifle away and idle away your time, really makes life demand of you hard work in other fields also. A high school athlete has more influence on ten, eleven and twelve year old boys than anyone else in the world. You are an example that they will always look up to and follow. Therefore, you owe the world a debt of decency in all that you do.

I trust that the future holds many good things for you and that you will find life both pleasant and profitable and that somehow or other, regardless of what troubles may come your way, you will always be able to look up to the stars.

Devotedly,

Coach Bill Story

Coach Bill Story

I received this insightful letter from Coach Bill Story at the time of his departure from Granby High School. As a parting thought, he reminded all athletes that they owe the world a debt of decency in all they do.

From the great football teams of Granby High School, which won three state championships and 32 consecutive games, there were three of us who went on to have notable careers in other sports. Chuck Stobbs, (left) and I played major baseball while Chauncey Willis, (right) won numerous titles in competitive sailing.

CHAPTER 5

"STRONG LEGS RUN THAT WEAK LEGS MAY WALK"

"Strong legs run that weak legs may walk." For me, this powerful motto, printed in the official game program for the first ever Oyster Bowl football game in 1946, became much more than just simple words on paper. As it was many years ago, it continues to be the familiar rallying cry of the Shriners organization, a group dedicated to helping children suffering from burns and crippling diseases. I was just a 17-year-old football player, a senior at Granby High School, when these words struck a chord in me and ignited a flame of purpose for my life, which has never flickered, even to this day.

World War II was over and our nation, united and proud, was entering a new era of prosperity. The years of shortages, sacrifices and rationing were behind us and many, who for the first time had a few extra dollars to spend, were ready to celebrate and enjoy life. We were proud Americans who were aware of our exceptionalism in the world and it showed. There was a swell of pride at a national level to go along with an undeniable type of local, hometown pride that could be easily seen everywhere in almost every city and town throughout our 48 states. Radio was in its heyday and television was still in its infancy, so there is no great mystery about why more than 21,000 fans paid $2.00 each to pack Foreman Field in Norfolk to see a showdown between the best two high school football teams on the East Coast as they faced each other in the inaugural Oyster Bowl on the afternoon of December 7, 1946.

Looking for our 32nd consecutive win, the Granby Blue Comets had just finished a third undefeated season in a row, while our worthy opponents from northern New Jersey, the Mustangs of Clifton High School, also had an impressive record going into the game. Under the guidance of Coach Joseph Grecco, the Mustangs, like us, had an unblemished slate through the regular season and had lost only one game in the past two years. It was the records and reputations of the two teams, along with a long list of renowned star players on each side, that fueled the media frenzy and helped set the stage for what would be the most highly anticipated high school football game ever played in Virginia.

Nevertheless, lost in the scramble for tickets and the waves of pre-game hype, there was the underlying true purpose for this showcase event. The Oyster Bowl game and parade, along with all of its associated festivities, were all parts of a grand concept which was transformed into a reality through the planning and hard work of the Shriners of the Norfolk-based Khedive Temple. In addition, while thousands of eager fans lined up at the ticket windows at Foreman Field, it's safe to say that many who were there to witness the big game didn't fully realize the vital part each of them was playing in helping crippled children around the world. More than $50,000 was raised that day and everyone looking on was treated to a hard-fought defensive battle which lived up to its billing.

It was a 12-yard aerial from Granby halfback Chuck Stobbs to our talented receiver, Barney Gill, in the opening quarter that staked the Comets to a 6 to 0 lead. Barney broke free from his defenders and caught the pass several yards shy of the goal line to set up what would be the only score of the game for either team. Despite allowing that early touchdown, Clifton was an even match for our squad the rest of the way.

The Mustangs pushed us to our limit on several occasions but never made it to the end zone. Three times the New Jersey boys forced their way deep into Granby territory and lined up with first and goal-to-go opportunities, and each time they came away empty-handed. Our defense seemed to play its best football in situations like those, when our backs were against the wall. Each time Clifton worked the ball inside our 10-yard line, they were turned away by our stingy defensive line, which showed the huge crowd how tough we could be and why we had not been defeated since 1944. Our head coach, "Snookie" Tarrell, had worked hard to prepare us.

Some of the late-game miracles performed by the Comets would not have been possible were it not for the superb pass coverage by our scrappy, 152- pound defensive back, Bobby Skinner. It also took a few bone-jarring tackles by our linemen to go along with Skinner's exceptional play to stall the final Clifton drive. This last push by the Mustangs ended when we took possession of the ball on downs, inside our one-yard line. It had taken our team's best defensive effort of the year to preserve the narrow lead and to make that victory the greatest sports moment in the history of Granby High.

The victory energized the entire Tidewater area of Virginia. There were press conferences and dinners to attend with cameras flashing and reporters hurriedly scribbling notes. The scene took on a storybook atmosphere for our team, but our period of jubilation could not be enjoyed for long, as our win in the Oyster Bowl had earned us a chance for even greater glory. With this victory we had secured an invitation to face an even stronger opponent in a game for the National High School Championship in the Orange Bowl in Miami in just a little more than two weeks.

After so many years... my personal mementoes from the greatest victory in the history of Granby High School

But during those days of celebration, immediately following the Oyster Bowl, I heard more and more about the money that had been raised by the event. I learned directly from some of the gentlemen who had worked hard to organize that game, just how important their work was and how much good it was doing. Even at that young age, I was drawn to appreciate the work of the Shriners and I learned how the futures of children less fortunate than I often depended on the efforts of that organization. Even then, I knew I needed to get involved.

For what would be the biggest football game ever for the Granby Blue Comets, we would have as our formidable opponents, the Rams of Lynn Classical High School, a school known for its powerful athletic teams hailing from Lynn, Massachusetts. The showdown scheduled for Christmas night drew almost 20,000 to the Orange Bowl, including many collegiate players from The University of Tennessee and Rice University. These fellows had arrived in town early to prepare for the Orange Bowl Game to be played on New Year's Day.

While Lynn Classical had a reputation of crushing all opponents in relentless fashion and the record to back it up, we were never intimidated by anything the sports reporters had to say. With only a day or two before the game, odds makers had tagged Lynn as a 6-point favorite, but that did nothing to stall our confidence. Coach Tarrell didn't hesitate to remind anyone who would listen that we were the team with the 32-game winning streak, not them!

The Lynn Classical team featured an extremely gifted athlete at quarterback who would go on to become one of the most beloved sports figures ever from the New England area. "The Golden Greek," as he was known, was Harry Agganis, a tall, 180-pound left-handed passer, the pride of The Bay State. Our squad had heard a little about the talents of Agganis from teammate Chuck Stobbs, who had played baseball with Harry earlier that year in the Esquire All-Star

Game in Chicago. Chuck had already warned us to be ready to face one of the best.

Much like the Oyster Bowl in Norfolk, this game was also promoted under the noble slogan, "Strong legs run that weak legs may walk." It was called the Annual North-South Shrine Football Game and Pageant and was sponsored by The Shriners of The Mahi Temple of Miami. Yet, with the mounting excitement of our train trip to Florida and the anticipation of playing in this important game, I again found my attention drawn to the cause of the Shriners and to the selfless effort they put forth for the benefit of others. I was impressed by the members I had met and couldn't help but notice their integrity, as well as the enthusiasm each of them had for the cause. They were a tight-knit band of brothers and I continued to think that someday I would like to join them.

After the overnight train trip from Norfolk, we were shocked by the warm weather waiting for us in Miami. But we quickly adjusted and found that our workouts in the Orange Bowl were a lot more to our liking than the final practice sessions we had back home. It was a totally new experience for us, practicing in the warm Florida sunshine and realizing that we were only a couple of days away from Christmas.

With so much at stake for both schools, it was expected that the boys on each side would have to deal with nervousness and pre-game butterflies to some extent. But for a team that was favored to win, Lynn Classical didn't do much to hide their jitters. After winning the coin toss and opting to receive the opening kickoff, the Rams fumbled on their first play of the game and turned the football over to us, deep in their territory. Yet, when we got our hands on the ball for the first time our first offensive drive sputtered and stalled without us picking up a first down. Even then, the game was taking on the signs of becoming a rough physical contest as there was fierce audible contact being heard on every tackle and block on every play.

On a later drive in the opening quarter, Chuck Stobbs intercepted the first of Harry Agganis's passes to give Granby possession of the football again and another opportunity to move into Ram territory. But again, our offense faltered. After being forced to punt, Classical took over on offense and resorted once more to the passing skill of Agganis. On the first down play, Harry went for his second pass attempt. While catching a glimpse of the ball as it sailed over the middle of our defense, I leaped into the air and snagged it with both hands for another Comet interception. Struggling to maintain my balance, I somehow managed to keep possession, then picked my way through several would-be tacklers and carried the ball across the midfield stripe to the Rams' forty-five yard line.

Again on offense, we had almost half the length of the field left to go before reaching the end zone and in the glare of the bright stadium lights, the goal posts looked as if they were miles away. On our next try, Chuck Stobbs hurled a long pass downfield and connected with halfback Barney Gill, who took the ball forward to the seventeen-yard-line. Suddenly at this point the goal seemed to be within our range.

The chains were moved and we started with a fresh set of downs. On first down the ball was handed off to our fullback Jack Lucas who bulled his way through the middle of the line, shaking loose first one defender and then another. Determined to break free, he continued to force his way forward until he was pulled to the ground on the two-yard line. Just shy of the goal, Jack carried the ball again and ground out the short yardage needed to break through the plane of the goal line, giving us the first score of the night. The Comets broke the ice in what had been a hard-fought defensive struggle up to this point. On the extra point attempt, I booted the football between the uprights to give

Granby a 7 to 0 advantage just seconds before the end of the first period.

On the ensuing kickoff, we forced the Rams to start deep in their own territory at about the 12-yard line. However, they didn't allow poor field position to hamper their offensive output. Classical ball carriers were able to string together gains of seven and eight yards, down after down, which eventually resulted in a game-tying touchdown. From a physical standpoint, this game was proving to be the most punishing and hard-hitting contest we had experienced. I spotted several players from each squad who were bloody or hobbling or slow in getting back on their feet. By playing at the middle of the line on both offense and defense, I was positioned at the center of much of the violence. And while some of the contact was nothing more than good aggressive football, several vicious hits by the Classical defense were late or made out of bounds and resulted in penalties for unsportsmanlike conduct, roughing the passer and unnecessary roughness.

Before halftime we answered the Classical scoring drive with another of our own. Using a consistent ground attack, we drove our way to the Rams' 30 for another first down. From there, Stobbs dropped back to launch a pass downfield, which split the gap between two defenders and again found its way to our sure-handed receiver, Barney Gill. Barney was taken down at the six-yard line. Yet because of another unnecessary roughness penalty against Classical, the football was moved half of the distance to the goal and spotted at the one yard line. Halfback Larry Brown, who had entered the game to replace Gill, then took a hand-off on the following play and squirted through the pile of tangled bodies and fell into the end zone for another Comet touchdown. Soon after another successful extra-point try, the second period ended and we headed to the locker room with a seven-point half-time advantage, a lead that would be short-lived.

We will never know what Coach Bill Joyce said to his boys during the intermission, but his pep talk sure proved to be an inspiring one for Classical. His suddenly rejuvenated Rams took the field for the start of the second half like a fresh new team. For what was a series of brutal hard-hitting plays, they stopped us cold on our first possession and from there, set the tone for the remainder of the game. On an offensive drive spearheaded by Agganis, the Rams used an effective mixture of running and passing plays to force the ball into our end zone to tie the game with little more than four minutes having elapsed in the half. Even then, the high-impact, aggressive style of play by both squads showed no signs of subsiding. If anything, it seemed to intensify.

Henry Foiles, *Center*

Playing the middle of the line, I was at the center of much of the violence.

While playing on the defensive side of the ball and only minutes left in the third quarter, I came in from my linebacker position and landed a solid hit on Classical's ball carrier, George Pike. It was a solid hit, nothing dirty, but with football being a game of physical contact, played at a time when face guards were still a few seasons away, Pike emerged from the pile-up with a bloody nose. His busted beak kept him out of the game for a handful of downs and then he was back on the field, angry and wanting revenge. In retaliation for what he thought was an intentional cheap shot, he enlisted a teammate to do his dirty work for him and it wasn't until we were back on offense and I took my place at center that I learned that he had a hit-man waiting for me. The instant I snapped the football to start our next play, I found myself held in the grasp of a Classical lineman who had latched onto my shoulder pads. With his fingers reaching under the neckline of the pads, he got a good grip and pulled me forward. With no way to make this opponent release his hold, I was forced downward, face first onto his raised knee. My nose was flattened and I was knocked nearly unconscious by the blow. I was wobbly and dizzy and needed help from my teammates to make it to the sidelines. My ears were ringing and my vision was fuzzy, but I was alert enough to get a look at the guy's uniform number while I was being helped up from the turf. I needed a short breather to help get the cobwebs out of my head, but suddenly I became a man with a mission. I was anxious to get back in the game and settle a personal score. This big guard may have had a tag for being a tough one, but I wasn't about to let him build his reputation on me.

Once I made it back onto the field for defense, I spotted this same player down in his three-point stance, lined up on the Classical offensive line. I returned to my position at middle linebacker, but after just one play I determined that I would have to move up on the front line to get a shot at this guy. Back in the huddle, I told one of our linemen to change places with me for a couple of plays, a change that would put me in perfect position to exact my revenge.

We broke the huddle and went into formation. Now up on the defensive line I watched my nemesis line up across from me as Agganis started calling signals. The very second he noticed that someone different was facing him, a look of serious confusion covered his face. "Paybacks are hell!" I mumbled, as I looked directly into his eyes. I leaned in on all fours and shifted my weight forward. I dug my cleats into the ground, assuring myself of solid traction for what was my ideal chance to retaliate. Sure, I was aware that what I was trying would draw a flag from the officials, but at this point my blood was boiling. I was so angry I could hardly see straight and a roughness penalty or even ejection was of no big concern.

At the snap of the ball, I kept my body low and bolted straight ahead. I made no effort to penetrate the line or to force my way into their backfield. I saw that my opponent suddenly sprung up to a near erect posture, as if to block for a pass play. That was precisely what I wanted, as he had literally played into my hand. It was my turn to commit an illegal hold and grab his shoulder pads. It was with all the strength I could muster that I managed to pull him toward me and force his upper body downward onto my leg. It was time for him to take a strong dose of his own medicine. He groaned with agony when I forced my knee into his ribs, sending him to the ground in a pile. He writhed on the turf as I turned away and headed for the huddle. I saw that his face was contorted and was turning the color of a fresh sugar beet. No whistles, no flags. No harm, no foul. That's the way I saw it. And if they were watching, maybe that's the way the officials saw it too. Perhaps they felt it was time for a Classical player to end up on the wrong end of a vicious play.

What I would say was the defining moment of the contest came as time was about to expire in the third period.

We had picked up an additional 15 yards on still another unnecessary roughness call against the Rams and in spite of the yardage assessed on the penalty, we were still faced with a fourth down near midfield. Instead of punting the ball back to Classical, we attempted to go for a first down and resorted to a familiar pass play that had paid off on numerous occasions during the season. However, on this try, our tried and true pass combination of Chuck Stobbs to Barney Gill came up empty and the ball fell incomplete. Our failure to convert on this fourth down play put the football back in the hands of the Rams offense for the opening of the final quarter.

I'm sad to say the Blue Comets of Granby could do nothing to crack the goal line during the fourth period, while Classical was able to find one more kink in our armor. The Rams concluded their final scoring drive about midway in the quarter when Agganis connected on another touchdown pass which gave them their first lead in the game. As events unfolded, it would prove to be the only lead they would need. We had other chances to score before time expired, but the Classical boys held us in check, knowing we would turn to a passing attack with the clock in their favor. We had a string of incomplete passes, including a couple of accurate tosses by Stobbs which were dropped by some of our most reliable receivers. Then a heartbreaking interception while precious time was ticking away, helped to seal our doom. Following a strong defensive effort, we held the rams for four plays to give ourselves one last opportunity to score. Yet, with very little time remaining, the pressure of rushing our plays proved to be too much, as our last play, another deflected Chuck Stobbs pass fell to the grass as the final gun sounded. Coming so close to another touchdown in the final seconds made this 21 to 14 loss difficult to accept.

The Rams of Lynn Classical returned home as the victorious 1946 National Champions of high school football. Nevertheless, the Granby Comets returned to Norfolk, feeling not only the painful sting of finishing the year as the number two team in the nation, but also reeling from the effects of having experienced our first defeat in three seasons. Many of our boys were in shock. We didn't know how to react to a loss, since so many on our squad had known nothing but winning since they first entered high school. Our string of 32 consecutive victories had come to an end, but no one could have guessed that to be the case, based on the reception that awaited us when we returned home and stepped off the train. The locals, about 200 of them, welcomed us, cheering us and hailing us as "real champions" and "the best ever!"

There have been other written accounts of what took place on the field during the third quarter that night in the Orange Bowl. One author in particular described the hit I made on George Pike as if it were malicious and involved unnecessary roughness on my part. In this same recollection, there is mention of a verbal exchange at the line of scrimmage, an instance when there was boasting and name-calling involving an opposing lineman and me. But to set the record straight, there was no such bragging or exchanging of taunts as he described. No one on the field that night could have boasted about being selected for All-American or All-South honors for the season; as it should be noted, the selections for those honors were not announced for several days following the game.

Nothing lasts forever, not even the record-setting Granby football streak. Yet, just as our longstanding dominance in scholastic football ended, my personal involvement with the Shriners and the marvelous work they do was just starting to sprout wings. Working to assure that everything humanly possible is done *so that weak legs may walk* is a passion that continues to drive me and still no one knows when that wonderful streak will ever end.

Granby High — Probable Starting Line-up

Left to right—front: (26) Joe Baines, (23) Louis McLeod, (30) William Etheridge, (27) Henry Foiles, (33) Chauncey Willis, (13) Buddy Lyons, (32) Dick Ivanhoe.

Back row: (17) Dickie Harrison, (18) Chuck Stobbs, (38) Jack Lucas, (25) Barney Gill.

CHAPTER 6

MY BROTHERS IN THE GAME

Professional baseball followed closely on the heels of my high school graduation and after several whirlwind seasons in both the major and minor leagues, I realized that time was passing quickly and I still had not acted on my urge to work with the Shriners and join their noble cause. However, at each stop in baseball, on each club, whenever I met a Mason who was a teammate or encountered a ballplayer who was a Shriner, I found each of them to be a person of strong character and I was intrigued by both the workers, as well as their work.

It was in November 1958 and about two and a half years had passed since the Cleveland Indians had dealt me to Pittsburgh. Soon after joining the Pirates, I found that there were at least 11 men with the ballclub, including our popular radio play-by-play man, Bob Prince, who were Freemasons. From a baseball standpoint, the group was a diversified one, which included players from almost every position on the field, plus one of the club's finer coaches, Sam Narron. The list included pitchers Bob Porterfield, Bob Friend and Ronnie Kline; outfielder Bill Virdon; and our shortstop and captain, Dick Groat. I had told myself before the schedule ended that I needed to set aside time during the upcoming off-season to begin the steps of initiation. So, it was with a lot of desire and determination that my life as a Mason and Shriner got started in the winter of 1958-1959.

Before a man can become a Shriner, he must first attain the degree of Master Mason, which is no small accomplishment in itself. I had a good idea of how much time and attention would be needed to get to that level and by this point in my baseball career I knew how quickly my off-season would fly by. With encouragement and offers to help coming from local Masons, I finally got down to business and submitted my application for the degrees of the Masonic order. It was with Owens Masonic Lodge No.164 AF & AM that I was initiated as an Entered Apprentice on November 20, 1958. That event only marked the beginning of a lot of hard work. For the first time since my school days, I found I was putting my study skills and my good memory to the test. Just as it is for the Masonic Apprentice today, working with a proficient coach can have a strong bearing on the time and ease with which he can advance. I was fortunate to have worked with a great coach and an old friend, Captain Jack O'Reilly. He was the ideal coach for me, a fine gentleman who had the patience and understanding that was needed to see me through the initiation process. I think back today as I work with some of my new brothers and hope that I can somehow do my duties as a coach as well as Captain Jack performed his. It was with his help over a period of less than two months that I completed my apprenticeship and was passed to the degree of Fellow Craft on the evening of January 15, 1959.

The holiday season was over and the time for leaving for spring training was quickly approaching. Personally, the time in between had been a period of intense study, training and memorization. Before my work to attain the level of Master Mason could be completed, a total in excess of 31,000 words would have to be spoken by me or on my behalf throughout the process. My time to get there was tight, but I knew with my memory skills and my enjoyment of a challenge, I could do it.

In spite of being pressed for time, I successfully stood the Master Mason's catechism on January 29, 1959, which left me with about two weeks to prepare for my annual trip to Fort Myers, Florida, for the Pirates' spring training. During the long drive I can recall anticipating how training camp that year would be special, a little different from the others. For the first time in my career, I was looking forward to seeing the other Masons on the ball club, especially Bob Porterfield, a Master Mason who had been very supportive and encouraging. This would be my first season with my new brothers in the game.

One of the most popular coaches ever to wear a Pirates' uniform was Samuel Woody Narron, a country boy from North Carolina who was Pittsburgh's bullpen coach for fourteen seasons, a stretch that saw him serve under four different managers. Sam was the sort of fellow who got along well with everyone and I would daresay that one would have to search long and hard to find anyone who had a negative word to say about him. He was the happy-go-lucky type who always enjoyed a laugh, even when it was at his expense. And heaven knows the man was given a lot of opportunities to laugh at himself.

He was born and raised in the heart of tobacco land in the tiny town of Middlesex, North Carolina, a hard-to-see dot on the map, found smack in the middle between Wilson and Raleigh. The small town spans an area of roughly one square mile, much of which is flat and still undeveloped. In spite of his upbringing in such rural surroundings, Sam struggled with a condition which is not uncommon, a likely innate condition called ophidiophobia, or more commonly called, fear of snakes. In his case his fear of the slender wiggling reptiles seemed to have been very intense. There were stories that claimed Sam would have shimmied up a tall tree or broad-jumped across a four-lane highway to stay clear of one!

Sam first saw action in the big leagues as a catcher when he joined the Gashouse Gang, the popular but rowdy St. Louis Cardinals, for a cup of coffee in 1935. It would be safe to say that there were numerous incidents going back to those days when he was a rookie and even before, when he was made the target of pranks and cruel jokes involving snakes. Often players would go to great lengths just to get a laugh on Sam, placing a live snake in a package and having it delivered to him or hanging a rubber serpent in his locker. Other times it could be something as simple as tossing a short length of electrical cable in the floor by his feet, which would cause him to jump to the ceiling. And though these tricks came at him in so many forms, he never lost his temper or let anyone know just how much he was tormented. He was a delightful fellow.

With a little bit of time on our hands, several of us were lounging in the Pirates' clubhouse when our discussion veered away from the usual talk about the headlines on the *Post-Gazette* or the best spot in town for dinner to the Masonic rings that some of us were wearing. Each of the rings in our group was beautifully designed in gold, with smart ornate patterns around a colored stone, with the well-known emblem of Freemasonry at its center. Compliments were being passed around among the fraternal brothers as each of us found something to admire with each ring. Suddenly it became obvious that there was one of us who was not wearing a Masonic ring, a traditional item which is known as one of the more accepted means of recognition among members. We all agreed that something needed to be done to correct this indignation, especially when the member without a ring was one of the finest fellows in the room, Coach Sam Narron.

The same baseball players who are capable of playing a cruel joke on a friend can also be very clever and creative whenever the time comes to do a good deed and pull off a secret undercover operation. That's exactly the type of plan we put together when the Masons of the 1959 Pirates' ballclub set out to get Sam a ring of his own. One of the fellows had connections with a local jewelry dealer and could get us the best price. Another of the guys had the most ingenious plan for gift wrapping. And all of us had suggestions about what style and which stone to order.

It must have been Bob Friend or maybe Ronnie Kline, one of the real wise guys, who handled the wrapping job, because it was his crazy way of packing and wrapping that added to the fun when our gift was finally presented to Sam. The ring was first fitted in a small box, wrapped and placed it in a slightly bigger box. It was then neatly wrapped again and packed in a still larger box and so on. The process was repeated until as many as eight or nine gift boxes had been wrapped, one inside of another. The last wrapped box, complete with bows and ribbons was large enough to have contained an entire case of champagne!

The brother Masons on the team came together when the colorful package was placed on a chair in front of Sam's locker. Once he learned that the surprise package was waiting for him, the look on his face told everyone that he was expecting the worst. For protection, he grabbed a bat and began taking short cautious steps toward his locker. He was unsure about what he would find, but he was convinced that it involved a snake. He nervously walked up to the package and started to examine it from a safe distance. Suddenly, he moved his hands down the handle of the bat and raised it above his head. He began to club the wrapped present, wanting to annihilate any living thing that could be inside. He struck several powerful blows, swinging the bat like a woodsman chopping a log.

"Take it easy, Sam!" one of the fellows urged him.

"There's nothing in there that'll hurt you," another assured. But Sam wasn't taking any chances. He had been victimized too many times in the past to trust ballplayers. By this time, the package was squashed and what had once been an attractively wrapped present looked a lot like a big pancake! "Okay, fellows," Sam conceded, "I'll take your word for it this time. But, if there's a snake inside that box, somebody will pay dearly!"

The room grew strangely quiet as he lowered the bat and leaned it against his locker. He inched closer and closer to the chair. He tentatively tugged on the smashed wrapping paper and ribbons. He was still nervous and not sure of his safety, but he decided to proceed. The onlookers were silent as Sam continued with his work, but the unusual quietness of the clubhouse only added to the suspense. He tore away the first box only to find another. He began to walk away from the chair, having second thoughts and not wanting to play along. But he was quickly coaxed back. "There's no snake in there, Sam, I swear to you," someone in the group assured him. "Just rip into it!" suggested another.

Sam continued, box after box with a little more assurance than before. He finally reached a tiny box that was much too small to hold a snake, even the smallest of species. So he stepped back onto the pile of crumpled wrapping paper and breathed a sigh of relief. He had arrived at the final cube, a box not much larger than a box of matches. Still anxious and with no clue about what to expect, he shook his head in frustration and took in a deep breath.

He carefully tore away the shiny paper, exposing the small velvet covered case which had been hidden inside. He flipped open the top of the case, exposing one of the most beautiful gold Masonic rings any of us had ever seen. Not a word was spoken while Sam slipped it onto his finger and raised his hand to show off his new prize. He was touched by the emotions of the moment. The Pirates' club house, which was sometimes loud and rowdy, was filled with an air of quiet tribute. Tears welled up in Sam's eyes. At that point he knew for sure just how much his brothers in the game admired and respected him. It was a special moment for him and for all of us. We had done something really nice for a really good man.

The world lost Sam Narron a few years ago, yet his legend lives on in baseball. He has two descendents who remain active in the game, his grandson, Samuel Franklin (Sam) Narron, a tall left-handed pitcher currently with the Milwaukee Brewers, plus former big league catcher, Jerry Narron, now a coach, also with the Brewers. Sam's son, Richard "Rooster" Narron is another in the bloodline who showed a strong leaning towards baseball. In addition to being the father of young Sam, the pitcher, Rooster was a baseball star at East Carolina University and is enshrined in the school's Athletic Hall of Fame. He also received All-American honors in 1967 while playing for ECU. Following a career in the minor leagues, he continues to reside in Goldsboro, North Carolina, where he is an active member of his community's lodge. Once the golden ring is spotted on Rooster's hand, no one can doubt his affiliation with the Masons. Everyday he wears this beautiful old ring which has never lost its luster or the tale of its origin. And Rooster would proudly share with you the same story I just told, about how it was presented to his father more than fifty years ago.

In addition to rings, which continue to be quite popular among members, other pieces of jewelry that carry the emblem of Freemasonry or The Shrine have been worn as items of recognition over the years. Lapel pins are another means of identification, which have been around for a long time and are still frequently seen today. As a baseball player on the go, traveling from city to city, I never went anywhere without first checking to be sure that my Shrine pin was fastened in place on the lapel of my sportcoat. It was a sharp-looking little accessory that I was proud to wear and in many cases it led to unexpected introductions and conversations with people I didn't know. But without a doubt, the most memorable introduction I can recall, which was a result of my wearing the pin, occurred in the clubhouse of the Los Angeles Angels, just after a game back in 1963.

Coach Sam Narron (left) is shown passing on some of the finer points of catching to Smokey Burgess and me as Coach Cal Ermer (right) looks on.

Most of the fellows had showered and dressed and were about to leave for the evening but I needed to hang around and ask some of my teammates for suggestions that could help me find a place to live. Having recently been released by the Cincinnati Reds and signed as a free agent by the Angels, I was still one of the newer players on the club and needed help with finding a suitable apartment or hotel in town. The ideal solution would be for me to find one of the players who could take on a roommate. With my wife Joyce and my two sons, Hank and Marc, back home in Virginia, I knew sharing a place with another player would be a lot better than living alone and would surely cut down on expenses. I was chatting with my old friend, Paul Foytack, a right-handed pitcher from Scranton, Pennsylvania, who I had first teamed up with a few seasons earlier in Detroit. I learned that Paul was living alone in a comfortable, yet affordable, hotel in Inglewood, across from Hollywood Park Race Track and he just happened to be looking for a roommate. He had just invited me to drop by and check out his place when I was distracted by a strong familiar voice coming from the far end of the clubhouse.

"It's The Cowboy coming through," I heard one of the other players say to another. I turned from my conversation with Paul and looked across the room to see what the commotion was all about. It was Gene Autry, America's most famous Singin' Cowboy, also the owner of the Angels, making his way through the room greeting players, all by name, shaking hands and making small talk. Wearing his white Stetson hat and his usual colorful Western-style shirt, it was unmistakably the hero of so many cowboy movies I had watched as a boy. Then in his mid-fifties, he still looked fit and trim, as if he were ready to jump on his horse Champion and chase down a gang of bad guys. He was friendly and outgoing. He seemed at ease, greeting everyone with a friendly smile.

Paul and I paused to watch as he continued to make his way through the clubhouse, but the people around him made it difficult. Suddenly, one of the players called for my attention. "Hey, Hank, he's over at your locker," he said in a quiet voice. That's all it took to get me heading in that direction.

"Whose locker is this?" he inquired as I got closer. He looked up at the top of my locker, to a place where a player's nameplate would normally be displayed. "I don't see a name here," he continued. "Is this locker for one of our new guys?" He took a look around to see if he could find a new face.

"Yes, sir, Mr. Autry," I chimed in. "It's mine. I'm Hank Foiles and I guess I haven't been here long enough for them to get me a name plate."

"Well, that's fine, Hank," he replied as he stepped forward to shake my hand.

"I couldn't help but notice the sport coat, hanging in your locker and the pin on the lapel. Is the coat yours, Hank?" he asked.

"Yes sir, it sure is," I responded, pleased to see that the tiny pin had caught his eye. Without releasing my hand, he continued our conversation.

"Welcome to Los Angeles, Nobel," he offered. "I realize that you haven't been in town long, so if there's anything I can do to help you find a place to stay or to help you get settled in, just give me a call. I'd be happy to help, Hank," he assured. "Just let me know."

"Thank you, thank you very much, Mr. Autry," I responded, wanting to make a good first impression.

"Don't forget, Hank, if there's anything…" he repeated as he stepped away.

The next time you're lucky enough to take in an Angels' home game, be sure to take a look at the row of retired numbers displayed beyond the outfield wall. Several of the numbers from Angels' history are quite recognizable. You'll easily pick out the retired uniform numbers for greats like Nolan Ryan's number 30 and 29 for Rod Carew. But, many fans are not aware that one number among the group of honorees was not retired as a uniform number. Number 26 is displayed to honor the team's great owner, the late Gene Autry, who cleared the way for the Angels to become a major league team. Without his dedication and his love of baseball, the second major league franchise to come to Los Angeles would never have been a reality. The beloved Cowboy Gentleman, president and owner of the team for almost four decades, was often referred to as the extra man on the club. He was known as the 26th man, with a team roster of 25. As the leader of the Angels' organization, he inspired everyone who worked for him to exceed even their own expectations. It was an honor to be his employee and I am proud to have known him as a brother in the game.

CHAPTER 7

WILLIE MAYS AND THE BATTLING PALMS

It really wasn't that long ago when professional athletes didn't make the outrageous salaries that they command today. And over the years as Major League Baseball led the way, paying the highest individual contracts, many of the game's biggest stars had to find offseason work to help carry them over financially from October until April. Prior to the era of free agency, it was not uncommon for an established big league ballplayer to join the work force as a salesman, a construction worker or even as a seasonal employee at an industrial plant. While today's baseball players spend much of their offseason working out with their personal trainers, the major leaguers of yesterday went to work. It was out of necessity that many of us got up by an alarm clock every morning, grabbed a lunch pail and rode into town to punch a time clock. Yet, for a few months each year as we rejoined the ranks of the conventional wage earners, it caused us to have a deeper appreciation for our jobs in baseball and made us all long for the opening of spring training.

For many, the ideal way for a pro ballplayer to remain gainfully employed during the offseason would be to have a gig that keeps him close to the game. For me, nothing was better than earning a little extra cash by playing in some local exhibition games.

When I returned home after getting my first "cup of coffee" in the Major Leagues, I was offered a chance to join up with a team of other professional players from around the Tidewater area of Virginia. With no official team name and a handful of exhibition games which were scheduled to start immediately after the regular season, this talent-laden bunch had quite a few recognizable names on its roster. With current major league players like veteran catcher Clyde McCullough, Red Sox infielder Allen Richter and pitching stars Chuck Stobbs and Bob Porterfield, there was no doubt that we could show the fans an exceptionally high level of play and draw some large crowds to watch.

The most formidable of opponents for our team of all-stars was a ball club of highly skilled African-American players named the Battling Palms, who also hailed from the Tidewater area. These fellows were both talented and experienced and were always ready to give us a run for our money, every time we squared off. Our weekend contests with the Battling Palms were a lot of fun for everyone involved and we soon found that the popularity of the games was spreading and a big following of fans was coming out for every game. We worked together with a standing agreement which called for the two clubs to split all gate receipts evenly. We soon found that our profits were steadily increasing along with the ticket sales.

During the course of this friendly rivalry, we learned that Willie Mays, the sensational young centerfielder of the New York Giants, was in the process of fulfilling his military obligations and was stationed at near by Fort Eustis, Virginia. Willie had been assigned to the United States Army Transportation Corps, yet he spent much of his time playing weekday baseball games for the installation's own military team, the Fort Eustis Wheels.

By having a baseball player with such notoriety and talent in our local area, the management of the Battling Palms saw a chance to cash in with Willie and further enhance our already profitable arrangement. No doubt, he could be the marquee player, who alone would be worth the price of admission. With Willie Mays playing for the Battling Palms, it would be a win-win situation for both teams as well as for the fans. It was good news to hear, after just a couple of days of ironing out the details, that Willie would be joining us for our next weekend match up.

With Willie in the lineup, we saw an immediate upswing in the attendance figures. His presence was a big drawing card for all types of baseball fans. Both males and females were coming out in droves to see him play. Regardless of their age or race, they cheered him for everything he did on the field. The stands erupted with noise each time he swung his bat, ran the base paths or made a catch. The fans seemed to hang on his every move.

Fulfilling his military obligations, Willie Mays was stationed at near by Fort Eustis, Virginia.

On a sunny autumn afternoon in front of a noisy packed house, we were in the early innings of a nip and tuck game against the Battling Palms when our manager Ray White popped out of the dugout. He asked for time and strolled slowly out to the pitcher's mound for a short meeting. Curious to find out what was on his mind, I came out from behind home plate to join in the conference. I pulled my catcher's mask away from my face and slid it back on my head.

Now White was a clever baseball man with many years in uniform. Years before he had been a crafty pitcher in the New York Yankees' farm system, and later he managed the Norfolk Tars, one of several Yankee teams he had played for. As I walked towards the mound, I noticed that Mays was kneeling on the on-deck circle and with him due up as the next batter, I figured he could be the reason for any defensive strategy Ray may have in mind. Instead of first speaking to the pitcher, as is customary when a manager steps up on the hill, Ray first turned to me to share his idea. I was a little surprised when he got around to making his proposal.

"You know, Hank," he began, "we have a pretty big crowd out here today. Let's give 'em what they came here for. Let's let Willie hit one outta here. That way, they will all go home happy and they'll all be sure to come back next Sunday for more of the same!"

I raised my eyebrows in disbelief as I stood there staring at Ray. The sound of his crazy plan had me puzzled at first, but then I started to recognize the financial side of the scheme. From that point of view, it made darn good sense. Ray had a good idea. Sure, it would be great to come away as winners in these exhibition games, but a fatter paycheck would be great, too!

"Here's what I want you to do, Hank," Ray continued. "When Willie comes up to bat, I want you to tip him off....Yeah, that's right. I want you to tell him what kind of pitch is coming. That way we can give him a little bit of an edge. I'm sure, if he were to smack a homer, this place would go (bleeping) nuts!"

The home plate umpire started to make his way out to break up our huddle.

"Come on guys!" he shouted. "Let's break up this meeting of the Ladies' Club …we got a ballgame to play!"

I turned and headed back to the plate. I grabbed my mask and pulled it down, over my face and gave the straps a tug.

"I can't believe I'm gonna do this," I whispered to myself. "This is about the craziest stunt I've ever been involved in on a baseball field."

Mays stepped up to the batter's box as I squatted down to give my signal to the pitcher. A right-handed hitter, he took a couple of practice swings and dug his spikes into the dirt. He glared out toward the mound.

"Willie, I tell ya' what I'm gonna do. I'm gonna make it easy for you," I offered. "I'm gonna tell what's coming on every pitch so you can belt one over the fence!"

"You're going to do what?" he asked.

"I need you to trust me, Willie," I assured. "Just listen to what I tell you and you'll be trotting around the bases before you know it."

It was obvious that Willie didn't trust me for a moment. He continued to look out at the pitcher while mumbling something about how he had never heard of such a hare-brained stunt as this in his entire life.

Our plan to give Willie an advantage went sour with the very first pitch. Just as the pitcher started into his delivery I gave him an honest-to-goodness tip about what to expect.

"Okay, Willie," I alerted him. "Here comes a fastball."

Willie took an awkward, off-balance swing and missed the baseball by several inches. He shook his head in frustration and stepped out of the box.

"I'm just trying to help you, Willie," I reminded him. Just as the pitcher toed the rubber and went into his windup, I tipped him again. "Breaking ball's coming now, Willie, get ready for a curve."

Willie took another rip, striking only the lower portion of the ball. The result was a harmless high pop-up on the infield, near the bag at second base. An easy catch was made to end the inning. He slung his bat to the ground in disgust and spun around to face me as I was leaving the field.

"Don't go messin' with me anymore like that, Hank!" he shouted. "Just leave me alone and let me do my job," he demanded.

"'Just trying to help you, Willie," I said innocently. "I'm just trying to help."

We went through a similar routine the next time he came to bat. The more advice I gave him, the more anxious and distracted he became. He continued to flail at the ball, popping it up in foul territory or driving it down on the ground for a routine infield out. At subsequent at-bats, it was more of the same. His batting miseries continued as he grew even more rattled and leery of my advance notices before each pitch. Pitch after pitch he failed to make good contact with the ball. He appeared off balance and his stride was not on time. With each pitch he was barely getting a piece of the ball. Or in some instances, he was missing it entirely.

We learned a lot about Willie Mays that day. We found that in spite of his exceptional talent as a baseball player, he could not be counted on for pre-planned heroics. He neither wanted nor needed any extra advantages and he would not benefit from any unsolicited advice. Today, whenever we see Willie hit a long homerun or make a great catch in those highlight films, we can be certain he did it naturally. He did it on his own and he did it his way. Willie Mays, like the fictional Roy Hobbs, is without question a baseball superstar who can be deservingly referred to as "a natural."

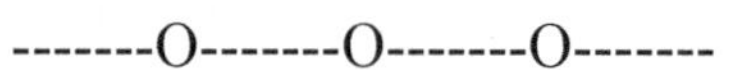

Maybe it was some sort of hex or spell that the New York Giants had cast on the Pirates just about the time I arrived in Pittsburgh early in the '56 season. Whatever our problem was, it was a chronic one. They beat us just about every way you can think of. And each of our losses seemed to be in some way due to the exceptional play of Willie Mays. Finding a way to stop Willie would be one of our challenges of the year.

After coming over from the Cleveland Indians in a trade for first baseman/outfielder Preston Ward, I didn't break into the starting lineup right away. For the first several games, Pirates skipper Bobby Bragan insisted that I keep a seat next to him on the bench. He claimed that I would pick up some valuable experience if I parked myself by him for a few days and studied the style of play. His purpose was to point out to me how baseball played in the National League was, what he called, "real hardball."

"This is real old-fashioned hardball over here in this league, Hank," he boasted. "You'll soon see a big difference between the caliber of play we have here, as compared to what you're used to. You won't find any of that country club kind of baseball here, like you played over there in the American League."

I didn't have to be seated next to Bobby or have the benefit of his many years in the game to see for myself that it was Willie, more than any other opposing factor that extended the Pirates' losing streak.

As the East Coast heat and humidity were starting to mount, we were struggling to complete the first half of our schedule. We were in fifth place by the midpoint of the season, playing at a near .500 pace. Our record at this point may have been a pleasant surprise for most Pirate fans. Yet, even in this spot in the National League standings, we found ourselves ahead of the Giants, who seemed to have a lot of difficulty winning games, except for the ones they had with us.

The Giants' train rolled into Pittsburgh for another late summer weekend set. This would be the typical four-game weekend series, which was not uncommon for that period. It began with a game on Friday night, followed by a single game on Saturday afternoon. The series would then conclude with a Sunday afternoon doubleheader. While the slightly cooler night air on Friday evenings could sometimes make those games tolerable, the oppressive dog days of summer could turn the day games on Saturdays and Sundays into long miserable affairs. Even though Forbes Field in Pittsburgh could be a tough place to play during a lingering hot spell, it was never as stifling as Sportsman's Park in St. Louis. But for me, after losing the first two games on Friday and Saturday to Willie Mays and the Giants and still having to play them twice more on Sunday afternoon, one place was just as bad as the other.

Before leaving my apartment that particular Sunday morning, I took a quick glance at the front of the morning newspaper. "HEAT WAVE CONTINUES" was all I needed to see before making a silent wish that I wouldn't have to catch both ends of the doubleheader. I also wished something could be done to cool this unrelenting weather.

Well, maybe it won't be too bad if we could pick up a win. But, to do that, we'll have to be at our best and we'll also have to find a way to cool Willie off, too.

I turned to notice the bright morning sunlight gleaming through my front window. Sleep had not come easily the night before as I had tossed and turned racking my brain all night for a way to slow down Mays's batting rampage. Getting back into bed seemed like a great idea, but I pushed myself to go out and face the day. Besides, it was getting late and hanging around that small stuffy apartment wasn't helping my disposition. I tossed the newspaper into the wastebasket and grabbed my sunglasses, just as I realized it was my day to drive. Teammates Bob Skinner and Danny Kravitz, who lived nearby, were already waiting by my car and neither said a word as I walked towards them, fumbling through my pockets for my keys. "No need to be in a rush, boys," I assured them. "The Giants will be ready for us no matter when we get there."

We drove out of the apartment complex in Valley View in South Hills and on to Sawmill Run Boulevard. It was an unusually quiet commute as I drove towards the Liberty Tubes. Fortunately, it was a Sunday morning and the freeway traffic was much lighter than normal. Otherwise it could have been a little scary for us, the way my mind was wandering back to thoughts of our nemesis, Willie Mays.

Staring blankly at the highway ahead, my mind began to drift. It wandered back into the not-so-distant past as I revisited a time a few years earlier when I was playing off-season exhibition games in Virginia and Willie Mays was a member of the Battling Palms. I thought about how he couldn't hit a lick as long as I told him what pitch was coming.

"Yeah, that's it!" I blurted out. My words may have startled the other guys after such a silent ride.

"What's it?" one of then asked. "What are you talking about?"

"Oh nothing," I answered sternly, not wanting to have my thoughts get untracked. "It's just a little something I've been thinking about."

I quickly reverted back to my idea, back to my deep level of concentration. I was struggling to decide if it was really worth bringing up. *Was it worth another try? It's an old idea that worked then, maybe it will still work now. Maybe we do have a way to cool Willie off, after all.* I stepped on the gas as we turned onto Forbes Boulevard. I needed to get to the stadium right away. I needed to have a talk with our manager Bobby Bragan as soon as possible!

The Oakland neighborhood was quiet as we drove closer to the ballpark. This thriving, mostly commercial section of central Pittsburgh showed no signs of its normal busy weekday activity. As I slowed down and turned into the player's parking lot, the summer sun was almost directly overhead. At this time of the day, even the tall massive exterior of Forbes Field did little to make shade from the broiling sun.

There were only a few players in the clubhouse when we walked in and I didn't take time to speak to any of them as I passed through on my way to the manager's office. It was still hours before game time, but of course Bragan was inside, seated behind his desk, getting an early start on his paperwork. With his reading glasses resting on the end of his nose, he looked up as I stood in the doorway.

"Good morning, Hank. You're here a little early today, aren't you?" he asked, checking his watch. "What's on your mind today?"

Once he spoke to me, I realized I may have distracted him just a little. His attention quickly went back to his papers before I could answer.

"Uh, yeah, Skip. I got this idea that I want to..."

Suddenly, I wasn't quite sure how to present my case. I didn't want him to think I had lost some of my marbles, so I started over again.

"Now Bobby, I know this may sound kinda crazy, but I think I might know of a way that we can keep Mays from beating us game after game."

Not having a clue about what I would say next, Bobby dropped his pencil from his hand and pushed his chair back from his desk. Totally lost and confused, he folded his arms, took a deep breath and peered at me over the top of his readers.

"What in tha'....? What are you talkin' about here, Hank?" he pried, needing some sort of explanation.

"What we need to do, Skip, is tip him off," I continued. "You know, let me tell Willie what pitch is coming."

My manager seemed to be even more confused than before. He needed more details.

I proceeded to give Bobby the full story, telling him about how I had played against Mays just a few years earlier and how the idea came about to have him tipped off before every pitch. I explained how, each time he came to bat, he swung as if he were handcuffed and how he was incapable of hitting the ball out of the infield.

Once I finished telling my wild story about Willie and the Battling Palms, Bobby sat quietly. He continued to stare at me as if I just arrived from another planet.

"You're serious about trying this, aren't you?" he finally asked. "You actually believe this scheme of yours could work again and keep him out of our hair?"

"Well, Skipper, I sure think it's worth a try and it certainly won't hurt anything," I assured him. "Look at it this way, Bobby," I continued. "What's Willie hitting against us now, about .999? So what do we have to lose? So what if he bats a thousand, will we notice the difference?"

My proposed plan had Bobby deep in thought. He stared down at the floor as he digested my story, giving it a moment of deep consideration before he finally looked up.

"Okay, Hank," he conceded. "Let's give it a try. It's like you said, what do we have to lose?"

With the early afternoon temperatures creeping up into the 90s and our strategic plan in place, the Sunday twin bill got under way. In the first game we found success against both Willie and the Giants. Not only did we grab a rare victory against New York, but Mays failed to reach base. With four unsuccessful trips to the plate, the only noise Willie could muster throughout the game was his high-pitched voice as he squeaked at me again and again, demanding that I stop telling him what pitch was coming next.

During the second game, it was easy to tell that our plan was paying off again. My good friend Ron Kline was our pitcher for game two and he had the entire New York batting order eating out of his hand. A tall right-hander from

Pennsylvania, Ronnie had a wide assortment of pitches which helped him forge a living in Major League Baseball for more than 17 years. He always managed to have good command of his fastball and slider and on occasions he displayed a pretty good change-up. However, the one pitch in his repertoire that even he would call substandard was his knuckleball. Ronnie knew that his version of the knuckler was virtually ineffective and he would never want to resort to using it in a critical situation. After recalling some of the great knuckleball pitchers, I caught throughout my career, I would tend to agree with him. While with the Orioles, I worked with the best of all knuckleball pitchers, Hoyt Wilhelm, and based on my experience with him, I can honestly say there are no others who can compare. Wilhelm's pitch had unpredictable movement, which could drive opposing batters crazy. Often his knuckleball would have the same effect on his catchers. I'll admit there were times when I thought his knuckler was going to drive me crazy!

Again, through the course of the second game, Mays continued to protest to home-plate umpire Augie Donatelli, pleading for him to put a stop to my verbal pitch calling. But Donatelli, a veteran National League umpire, who had seen almost everything during his time in the game, was suddenly forced into playing a role similar to that of a stern father, about to deal with his two bickering sons.

"Augie, make him stop talking to me!" Willie complained. "Tell him to shut up!"

"Oh, come on now, Willie," Donatelli responded in a calm parental voice. "He's not doing anything wrong. He's not using any bad language and he's not breaking any rules. I can't make him stop talking, so get back in the box, Willie, and let's play ball!"

"Well, that's just not right, Augie," Willie whined as he turned to resume his stance at the plate. "It's just not right!"

This was Mays's fourth trip to the plate in game two and so far, in this lopsided contest he had managed nothing more than to get himself thrown out at first on a weakly hit grounder and two harmless pop-ups. Surely, he was remembering how these same tactics from a couple of seasons earlier had worked against him and I could tell that his pot of frustration was about to boil over. The Pirates were holding a comfortable six-run lead and with the bases empty, we were just a couple of outs away from an unheard of doubleheader sweep of the New York Giants. I quickly assessed the situation and reasoned that if we were ever to have some fun with Willie, the "Say Hey Kid," now was the perfect time.

While down in my crouch position behind the plate, I rested my catcher's mitt on my left knee to conceal my signals as I looked out to the mound. When Kline leaned forward to see my fingers, I flashed the signal sequence which called for his knuckleball. Because Ronnie and I used this sign so infrequently, he paused to check again before he nodded his head in agreement. He held back a faint smile as he tapped the pitching rubber with the toe of his right shoe. Ronnie knew what was going on and he was ready to be part of the set-up.

"Are you any good at hitting a knuckleball, Willie?" I asked just as Kline started into his delivery. "You need to be ready, 'cause that's what's on the way!"

"Tell him to shut up, Augie!" he squeaked one last time.

Following the pitcher's release, the baseball floated in towards home plate. It was up, about belt high and stayed there as it got closer and closer to Willie. The ball had no jump, no movement at all. It was simply a slow fat pitch, out over the middle of the plate.

Willie had stopped talking only long enough to take a vicious cut. He stepped into the ball, got his arms extended and made a powerful, level swing. He made solid contact and the impact abruptly changed the directional path of the baseball. Crack! He sent it flying, high and deep to left-center field. It sailed over the ten-foot high outfield wall and finally returned to Earth some 450 feet away. Willie was delighted. His short-lived batting slump was over and he had the pleasure of ending it with a long tape-measure homerun. As he circled the bases, he glanced out to the distant bleachers where his blast had landed. The fans rose to their feet and applauded as Willie trotted methodically towards home. Donatelli reached into his ballbag and flipped me a new baseball. I took a quick look at it and tossed it out to Kline. Ronnie had stepped down off the hill and nodded his head from side to side as he snagged the new ball. He was trying hard to suppress a smile.

Willie stepped on the plate and paused for a moment before heading to the dugout. He reached out and grabbed my hand. He looked directly at my face and gave me a quick, unexpected handshake.

"Job well done, my man!" he chirped, in a voice barely loud enough to be heard above the cheers. "Well done!"

Today, I see his handshake as a gesture of gratitude, as a way of saying "thank you" from one professional to another. I believe that he knew deep within himself that we got the upper hand on him that hot Sunday afternoon, long ago in Pittsburgh. Even now, as Willie Mays holds the number four spot on the all-time career homerun list, I can say for sure that he had a little help with at least one of his of 660 homeruns.

CHAPTER 8

"EVIL EYE" CHARLIE DOUGLAS

For more than four decades newspaper subscribers all across the country were treated each morning to a heaping helping of the whacky antics of the folks from the backwoods Kentucky town of Dogpatch. It all came our way from 1934 until 1977 in the delightfully funny comic strip, *Li'l Abner*. Each day the storylines were spun around the bizarre and simple-minded assortment of characters that lived in the tiny mountain town. In most installments the plot spotlighted the ongoing romantic adventures between the main character, Li'l Abner and his voluptuous blond sweetheart, Daisy Mae. Yet there were other amusing residents of Dogpatch who made regular appearances in the strip and contributed their fair share of zaniness for the readers' amusement.

Evil Eye Fleegle, a seedy looking zoot-suiter from Brooklyn, New York, was one such character. As a villainous transplant from the big city, Fleegle was always up to no good. His calling in life must have been to play a role in any schemes of deceit and trickery, anything that could derail the hopes and good intentions of any of the decent folks among the hillbilly clan.

Fleegle was the possessor of a strange and unique talent. Through the use of his "evil eye," he had the capability of putting a "whammy" on anyone he chose. Once his evil eye was activated and its powerful beam of energy was projected at his target, the victim would be left motionless until the effects of the whammy wore off. But that was just his basic ordinary whammy. He also possessed other levels of the whammy, which were far more horrifying and destructive. For instance, there was the "double whammy" which was powerful enough to crumble a skyscraper. And then, the dreaded "triple whammy" which could melt a battleship! In any event, the world has never seen a more devastating spell or a more powerful hex than the terrifying whammies of Evil Eye Fleegle.

The baseball season of 1957 brought with it another chapter in our ongoing feud with the contentious New York Giants. It was my second of four seasons with the Pirates and would prove to be one of my most productive and memorable years in baseball. However, other than an opening day win over New York at Forbes Field, we had had little success against New York. Yet to some degree, we were still able to curtail the offensive production of the great Willie Mays by simply resorting to the same tactics we used to throttle him in Pittsburgh a year earlier. The routine was starting to become familiar. Whenever he stepped up to bat, I needed only to mumble a few words to break his concentration. The slightest little quip from me was all that was needed to unnerve him. His ongoing hitting slump against the Pirates had Giants' manager Bill Rigney at the end of his rope. As the club's field boss, Billy was too attentive to his work not be aware of what we were doing to his all-star slugger, and he was determined to put a stop to it.

We had heard through the clubhouse grapevine that Rigney had counseled Willie and urged him to ignore anything I might have to say, especially whenever he was in the batter's box. But after seeing no positive results, the New York manager was forced to take further actions. After determining that I was at the root of Willie's difficulties, Rigney ordered Willie to have no contact with me. Under no circumstances was he to speak to me and he was to avoid being within earshot of anything I had to say. To back up his orders, Rigney also threatened Willie with a fine of fifty dollars for each occasion that he was seen conversing or fraternizing with any opposing players. Rigney was extremely upset about this whole matter and was ready to take measures to protect every player on his team. On the other hand, hearing about all of this spurred me on and caused me to search for still more ways to keep Mays on the hook a while longer.

With the all-star break right around the corner, the Pittsburgh Pirates of '57 were in the precarious position of having one foot in the grave and the other on a banana peel. We were more than twenty games under .500 and locked in last place in the National League. Yet our organization's brass was not ready to throw in the towel. To their credit, they pulled out all the stops, trying to salvage our dismal season. Orders were given to add some new arms to our already beleaguered pitching staff. At different points during the campaign an assortment of promising young right-handers were brought onboard to be tested at the big league level. After receiving their promotions to Pittsburgh, each of them was subjected to a baptism by fire and as a group, they all held up well under the pressure. Each of them did a commendable job. This group of hurlers, who were all new faces in the Pirates' clubhouse, included George Witt, Chuck Churn, Bennie Daniels and one of my all-time favorite teammates, Charles William Douglas.

Charlie Douglas was a thin, raw-boned right-hander who had several productive seasons in the minor leagues prior to his midseason call-up. He was a good-natured, likable country boy, just as you would expect for a young man from Carrboro, North Carolina. However, while growing up in that small town in central North Carolina, Charlie suffered a childhood accident which unfortunately caused him to loose his right eye. Yet with what would have been a major obstacle or even an excuse for some boys, Charlie, with his strong competitive spirit, never allowed his restricted vision to be a hindrance as he continued his pursuit of playing professional baseball. His artificial eye was never very noticeable, but you can imagine the amount of kidding he had to take from fellows who are as hard and insensitive as baseball players can often be. Ball players were the same no matter where I went. Regardless of the level or classification that I played, there were always guys on every team who were looking for something to rib one of their teammates about. The clowns and jokers on the '57 Pirates club had lots to feed on with Charlie's glass eye. Yet he always took it in stride and managed to laugh along with his would be tormentors.

Maybe it was when Charlie took the mound and stared in at his catcher to get a signal or maybe it was when he glared over his shoulder at a base runner who was taking a threatening lead. Either way, it was something about his menacing visual contact that caused some players to feel as if they were about to receive a "whammy." Since most ball players had enough free time to follow the comic strips, associations were soon made between Li'l Abner's Evil Eye Fleegle and our own Charlie Douglas.

Charlie Douglas was one of my all-time favorite teammates.

An ordinary tag like Charlie no longer seemed to be a good fit for him, so the name was dropped and forgotten. It went the way of Studebakers and stove black and soon he was known throughout the National League as simply "Whammy."

While working the first half of the season with Pittsburgh's minor league affiliate, the Columbus Jets of the International League, Whammy, a lanky Tar Heel turned in some impressive numbers. He won ten games over the short time span and carried a stingy earned run average of less than three. There were a lot of high hopes pinned to Douglas and some of the other rookie pitchers as the Pirates, who were not a wealthy team by anyone's standards, worked diligently to lay the groundwork for a brighter future.

The weeks rolled by and soon it was time to square off once again with the New York Giants. On this occasion the stage was set for a four-game series to be played at the Polo Grounds, the Giants spacious home in Upper Manhattan. For a few weeks we had all been hearing the rumblings about how the owner of that franchise, Horace C. Stoneham was making plans to uproot his team and head to the West Coast. The same ugly rumor was being circulated about the Brooklyn Dodgers owner, Walter O'Malley. Yet like so many other players around the N.L., I viewed the whole deal as a lot of threatening talk, which I wouldn't believe until I saw it happen. At the time of this Pirates-Giants series, I had no idea that this would be the final season for the Giants in their old East Coast home.

At the Polo Grounds, clubhouses for both teams were located upstairs beyond the centerfield wall. This arrangement made for a long walk to get down to the playing field once you got suited up for the game. On this day I had hardly reached the bottom of the stairs and stepped onto the outfield grass when I spotted Willie Mays across the field, standing near the portable batting cage at home plate. The Giants were starting their pregame batting practice as Willie stood casually by the backstop, waiting for his turn in the cage. He stood with his bat resting on his shoulder and peered out to the outfield. He appeared to be chatting through the screen with a teammate on the other side. But the conversation ended once he noticed that I was walking in his direction. Suddenly Willie looked down at the ground as if I were the last person on earth he wanted to see. Of course, I wasn't about to let him ignore me.

I needed to exercise caution before I took this situation any further. I could easily land myself in big trouble if I got caught throwing any more fuel on the fire, since stern warnings had already been issued by the league office concerning on-field fraternization among opposing players. The penalty, a fifty-dollar fine for each infraction, was the sort of thing a young catcher like me needed to avoid if at all possible.

As I walked to the cut on the infield grass, I got a glimpse of a couple of N.L. umps seated in the box seats directly behind the plate. They were sitting together in a single row of seats, lined up like hungry vultures sitting on a limb. This particular crew of umpires had been assigned to work the entire series with us in New York, but in this instance they were working like undercover police officers assigned to a stakeout. They sat quietly, listening and observing. They were trying to catch any of us who dared violate the fraternization rules.

Also in the area behind the batting cage was my good friend Jack Hernon, a writer from the *Pittsburgh Post-Gazette*. Jack was there with his ears open and his eyes pried in case there were any new developments in the Willie Mays–Hank Foiles saga. A juicy scoop about Mays would be good fodder for his column. Jack had been on top of the situation from the start. He had talked with me on a couple of occasions back in Pittsburgh and joined us on this road trip, waiting and hoping for the next shoe to drop. As things unfolded, he wouldn't be kept waiting for long. The moment

I discovered that none of the lookouts in the seats was watching, I began to stir the pot and yelled out to Willie.

"You need to be careful today, Willie," I warned. "We have a young kid pitching today who throws some real heat and he's as wild as a jack rabbit!"

Willie turned his back to me, hoping he could make me go away. It didn't help him at all, so I took another shot and continued my razzing.

"Yeah, he's wild, Willie,-and he can't see very well either!"

Wanting no conversation with me, he looked around nervously, first at the dugout and then towards the box seats. It was time for him to retaliate.

"Get away from me, Hank!" he ordered. "Don't be talkin' to me!"

His nervous reaction was exactly what I was wanting from him, but before I could close this case, I still had a few closing remarks left to make.

"Yeah, Willie, this young kid isn't trying to hurt anyone; he just can't see a wink. And watch his hands, too Willie," I advised. "If he waves his hand and motions for you to move closer to the plate, that means he can see you and you'll be okay."

Just as I redirected my path and veered off to the Pirates' dugout, I heard Billy Rigney yelling at Mays. "What did I tell you about that, Willie?" he scolded. "Now ignore that guy and get back to work!"

Only a few short steps from the bench, I took another look in the direction of home plate. I spotted Jack Hernon, who smiled and gave me a wink. He reached for a ballpoint in the front pocket of his white short-sleeved shirt and quickly scribbled a few notes on his pad. His interest had been awakened by the pre-game drama.

I found some room on the bench and dropped my bats and catcher's gear in a pile, next to where Whammy Douglas we sitting. I couldn't get him to look up at me as I stood beside him. He was busy tapping his feet on the dugout floor and chewing his fingernails. He had drawn the starting pitching assignment that afternoon and his nervousness was showing. I hoped that sharing a bit of pre-game strategy with him would take the edge off and help calm him down.

"Whammy, ol' boy, here's what we need to do today," I said, still trying to grab his attention. "Let's be sure to get the first two hitters out in the first inning, so when Mays comes up to bat the bases will be empty. 'You with me so far?" I asked.

He was quiet for a moment then he looked up at me with that penetrating glass eye. That's when I knew he was listening and ready to hear me out.

"When Willie comes up to the plate with two outs and no runners on base," I continued, "I want you to put a fastball inside on him, directly at his front shoulder. I want you to put him down in the dirt. Are you with me on this, Whammy?" I asked.

"Sure, Hank," he assured me. "I'm with you all the way."

I was satisfied that Whammy was ready to carry out the plan. He even seemed eager to get started with the prankish scheme. In spite of the short time he had spent in the National League, it was clear that he was willing to play the game the way Bobby Bragen preferred. My new battery mate from North Carolina was ready to play some good old fashion hardball!

"Now there's one other thing left for us to do, Whammy," I continued. "When Willie gets up off the ground and steps back into the batter's box, I want you to give him a signal with your hand. Just wave your hand to let him know that your vision is fine and that it's safe for him to get back in the box and step even closer to the plate."

A smile came to Whammy's face as he sat quietly and stared out at the field. Maybe he was contemplating his part in this crazy operation, but I wasn't quite sure. For a moment

I waited for a response and wondered if he had heard anything I had said. Finally he broke his silence.

"Okay, Hank, we'll make it work," he declared confidently. "But first we need to make sure we get those first two hitters out," he reminded me. "If we don't, then all bets are off!"

Within minutes, I noticed that Willie had stepped away from the batting cage and was over by the masonry wall which circled around behind home plate. I suppose that location was better suited for a private conversation than the noisy area around the cage. Willie was having a chat with Jack Hernon.

"Look, Whammy, won't you check that out?" I exclaimed. "Willie's taking the bait! Jack must've invited Willie over for a talk and now Willie is hearing the full story about you. And this time he's getting it from someone other than me!"

As luck would have it, we retired the first two Giant batters in the bottom of the first inning. As Mays, the third hitter in Rigney's lineup, left the on-deck circle and headed to the plate, I nodded to Whammy, reminding him that it was time to put all of our talk into action. Without drawing attention, Whammy nodded back, letting me know he was ready to follow through.

I squatted behind the plate and lowered my right hand between my legs and extended only my index finger, calling for a fastball. Even though this first pitch to Mays had been planned well in advance, Whammy nodded in agreement, as if everything was normal. Without a word from me, Willie cautiously entered the batter's box and took a short awkward practice swing. He was so hesitant and uneasy that it caused me to wonder if he suspected something was up. As Whammy toed the pitching rubber and started into his delivery, Willie took another rushed practice cut. Whammy's fastball was on its way.

In a fraction of a second, the baseball closed in on Willie. High and inside it came, as if it had been fired from a Howitzer. It was at least a foot off the inside edge of the plate and speeding straight for Willie's left shoulder. He had only one option and that was to bail out. Willie landed on his back in the dirt! His bat went sailing in one direction, his helmet in another. In a half-hearted attempt to catch the ball, I reached high to my left, but managed to only have it nick the top of my mitt before it went crashing into the screen behind home plate.

An eerie quiet fell over the crowd as they rose quickly to their feet. For several seconds Willie lay still on the ground, struggling to regain his senses. Of course, he was unhurt, yet obviously shaken. Finally, he moved, shifting his body and twisting his way to a sitting position. He looked like he was about to say something to me, but before he could talk, he first needed to finish spitting the dirt from his mouth. He never got the chance to speak before I started in on him once again.

"Don't look at me, Willie," I said, trying to sound innocent. "I tried to warn you!"

Willie rose slowly to his feet, retrieved his bat and helmet and began to brush away the dirt from his arms and the seat of his pants. He turned and glared at me as he stepped back into the box.

"Like I said, Willie, don't look back here at me. You need to look out there at the mound. The man out there is the one with the ball!"

At that instance Willie unwittingly took my advice and looked out at the imposing six-foot-two inch Whammy Douglas standing on the pitcher's mound. Whammy stared back at Willie and with a side-to-side hand motion, beckoned for Willie to stand in closer to the plate. By now Willie was as jumpy as anyone who had ever walked onto a baseball field. He mumbled a few indiscernible phrases to himself as he stepped up to the plate and nervously took another quick swing at the air with his bat. Not another word was spoken as he slowly and deliberately began to alter the landscape in the batter's box with his feet.

"Well, hell, Hank!" he finally blurted out. "Just tell him to go ahead and throw three, 'cause I ain't swinging at any of 'em!"

He eventually composed himself and stepped up to the plate. Yet with his bat cocked back, but resting lightly on his right shoulder, he proceeded to take three consecutive called strikes. Whammy delivered three perfect pitches, each one a fastball and each one right over the heart of the plate! Putting up no resistance Willie was the final out in the home half of the first inning.

He would go on to finish the 1957 season with the second highest batting average in the National League, but on that occasion, Willie was nothing more than the first strikeout victim of the afternoon for Whammy Douglas

I can't be certain, but it's possible that Willie Mays may have fallen victim that day to some sort of magical curse or maybe a spell. But most likely he had been subjected to some variation of an evil "whammy." And who knows, maybe it was a double or even a triple whammy, you can decide for yourself. Either way, one thing's for sure. This whammy was cast by a young right-handed pitcher named Charlie "Evil Eye" Douglas...not from Dogpatch Kentucky, but from Carrsboro, North Carolina.

When Charlie Douglas came to the Pirates, he was ready to play some good old-fashioned hardball!

CHAPTER 9

NOT ALL THAT GLITTERS IS GOLD

It's the twenty-first century, and for me, the world has changed more than I ever thought possible. Every day I am astounded by what's on television and by what I read in newspapers. The news headlines can tell about international events, politics or the nation's economy-- it makes no difference-- and they all give me reasons to wonder just how much longer this old planet of ours can keep spinning.

In today's markets, prices for everything seem to rise daily, while the cost of a secure, comfortable life is quickly getting beyond the reach of most hard-working Americans. And while our nation's unemployment is the highest it has been in more than 70 years, salaries for professional athletes have sky rocketed to unimaginable levels. With the agreement Alex Rodriguez signed with the New York Yankees a few seasons ago, he was paid more than $45,000 for each at-bat, almost the average annual income for an American household at the time.

Yet, there are so many unanswered questions about this entire arrangement, all which should lead us to speculate how and when it all got so far out of control. Possibly, it all started with the advent of player free agency or maybe it's because of the egotistical greed of today's players and their agents. Or perhaps it's the fault of the owners who obviously misplaced their sanity at some point along the way. Regardless, terms like player strike, player lockout, player's agent and free agent were never part of professional sports at any time during my career. Money has changed it all. In many ways baseball is a different business and a different game today. It's a different world today.

While playing high school and American Legion baseball, I drew the attention of several big league scouts. There was one such fellow in particular who worked for the New York Yankees in whom my father and I would ultimately place our complete trust, only to learn later that not all that glitters is gold.

His name was H. P. "Percy" Dawson, a long-standing figure in the Yankee organization who worked for them most of his adult life. Starting in the club's New York business office in the early '30s, Percy impressed Colonel Jacob Ruppert and his staff and was put to task wearing many different hats. His diligence paid off and he was soon given full charge of running the Yankees' class B team, the Norfolk Tars. In Norfolk he worked as both general manager and business manager for more than two decades. While I was in my teens, Percy stayed abreast of all of my athletic activities and over time gained the confidence of my family and me.

While working and living in Norfolk for many years, Dawson remained a good friend of Dad's. Their dealings went back to the days when the two had played baseball together in the old Virginia League. In later years, with Percy's line of work and my father's extensive baseball background, it was easy for them to continue their relationship. Both men possessed a good eye for assessing baseball talent and a keen business sense. On occasions Dawson was known to welcome my father's input in baseball, business matters and other shared interests.

After working out the particulars with his superiors in New York, Percy arranged for Daddy and me to fly to New York for a special workout, scheduled just for me, which would take place at Yankee Stadium. After accepting the invitation and arriving in the Big Apple, we soon found that

Percy's endorsement actually carried significant weight with his employers, as both Daddy and I were treated like royalty. For an entire week we were provided with the best of hotel accommodations and the finest meals. And while Daddy, who was never one to be awestruck, kept his focus on the business aspect of my audition, I was in a daze, like any other eighteen-year-old American male would have been. I was completely caught up in the excitement and thrills of having a tryout on the grounds of the most famous ballpark in the world, while some of the biggest stars in the game of baseball looked on. The entire experience was dreamlike.

After what we felt was a good showing in my tryout, we left New York feeling confident that our dealings with the Yankees were far from over. During our flight back to Virginia, Daddy assured me that the odds were pretty good that they would be making a contract offer sometime soon. Yet he also reminded me how vital it was to keep all doors open and to listen to all offers before entering a binding agreement with any team.

After returning home from our weeklong whirlwind trip to the Bronx, we soon got the word of more good news. It seemed that during the time of my courtship with the Yankees, the Brooklyn Dodgers had been developing a plan of their own. Rex Bowen, a well-traveled professional baseball scout was working for the Brooklyn Dodgers at the time and he, too, had made it a point to introduce himself after seeing me play a few games for Granby High and even dropped by the house to visit with my parents. He expressed a strong interest in me and seemed enthusiastic about the possibility of my signing with his club following my graduation.

But soon after finishing high school, I joined up with a semi-pro baseball team in Elizabeth City, North Carolina. At first, this was to be nothing more than a way of staying active in baseball during the summer while Dad and I anticipated hearing from other teams. However, it was there in North Carolina that I had a close call which could have jeopardized my chances of turning pro.

Early in the season I was involved in a close play at home plate, which resulted in a serious injury to my left knee and, as many of you know, a damaged knee can often be the kiss of death to a catcher's career. My season with Elizabeth City was finished and for several weeks I was on pins and needles waiting to learn my fate as a big league prospect. Fortunately, I made a full recovery and was sidelined only until August as my knee responded well to the rest and treatments. At last, after what had been a long stressful waiting period, the clouds of doubt that had been hanging over my career had finally lifted. It was such a relief when I finally learned that my injury had not dulled Bowen's interest in me. He was satisfied that my knee was healed and that it would have no effect on my future. To make things even more enticing, Rex arranged for my father and me to travel to Brooklyn for a trial workout at Ebbett's Field and a meeting with the Dodger's owner and general manager, Branch Rickey.

Compared to many other prospects, I had a big advantage having my dad with me whenever I met with scouts and executives from professional baseball. When it came to contract negotiations, Daddy was not just a shrewd business man who could turn a deal, but he had also been exposed to the business side of baseball long enough to know many of the pitfalls to avoid. He understood that baseball was a business, first and foremost, where the club kept its own interest as a priority, while all too often the best interest of the player fell as only a secondary incidental. You might say I had my own agent to represent me, during an age when a player having a personal agent or representative was unheard of and the concept was still many years away. From a legal standpoint he was permitted to speak with team officials on my behalf since he was my parent and because of my age, at eighteen I was still considered a minor.

Dad and I made it to Ebbett's Field in Brooklyn, New York, at a time when the Dodgers had all but sewn up the 1947 National League pennant. Also, it was there in Brooklyn where only months earlier, the club had made baseball history by signing a twenty-eight-year-old first baseman named Jackie Robinson. As the record books will confirm, this much publicized contract agreement made Robinson the first African-American to play Major League baseball. Yet, while he was aware of the tradition and significance of the grand old stadium and the notable role Mr. Rickey played in the landmark event, my father was not about to be won over by history and sentiment or be intimidated by anyone's famed reputation.

The Dodgers presented themselves as a first-class organization. They rolled out the red carpet and made every effort to make us feel at home. They put me through quite a lengthy workout, first, having me spend an extended time in the batting cage, followed by a series of defensive drills to test my skills behind the plate. My entire audition had been carried out under the watchful eye of coach Clyde Sukeforth. "Sukey," as he was often called, was a seasoned catcher who had toiled many seasons in the National League. But more recently, he had successfully finished a very critical mission for Branch Rickey and the Dodger organization. During the spring he played a key part in a covert plan devised by Rickey to help the Brooklyn club broker a player contract with Jackie, then a superstar in the Negro Leagues. He had been entrusted with the delicate job of secretly scouting Jackie on behalf of Mr. Rickey and persuading Jackie to return with him to New York for a meeting in Rickey's office. Robinson eventually inked his deal with the Dodgers in April 1947, and the rest is history.

With Sukeforth pitching batting practice, I was subjected to a grueling workout in the hitting cage. It was August and the sticky summer heat had taken a toll on me as well as the coach. "Okay, Hank," he finally offered. "Let's say that's enough for today and go get a shower."

His idea to end the workout had come none too soon for me. My scratchy wool flannel uniform was completely soaked with perspiration, which added on a load of several extra pounds for me to carry. I followed Coach Sukeforth to the dugout and into the tunnel leading to the clubhouse. The ex-catcher, still quite fit and agile for his mid-40s, seemed to be handling the oppressive temperatures as well or even better than I was. "Yes sir, Hank," he drawled in his distinct Maine dialect. "Let's relax for a minute and get a cold drink. Then we'll get a shower and go up to Mr. Rickey's office. He'll be expecting us up there shortly."

I couldn't help but notice the impressive gold leaf lettering on the frosted glass panel of the office door, *Brooklyn National League Baseball Club, Inc.* Sukeforth stepped ahead and slowly pushed the door open before quietly excusing himself. Daddy and I were greeted by a lovely young receptionist who offered us a seat in the waiting area as she reached for the switch on her desk intercom.

"Mr.Foiles and his father are here to see to see you, Mr. Rickey," she announced, speaking directly into the face of the black box. I hardly had time to pick up the latest copy of *Baseball Magazine* from the coffee table before we heard a response.

"Send them on in," the voice from the box directed.

Even before we had entered his office, Mr. Rickey had stepped from behind his massive ornate desk to offer us each a hearty handshake. "Welcome, gentlemen, it's good to see you," he offered. "I've been expecting you."

For a fellow in his mid-60s, he appeared to be even older than his years and with his trademark, stub of a cigar between his lips, I was suddenly taken by what were likely the thickest, bushiest eyebrows I had ever seen. He may have seemed a little slow and cautious when he turned and walked back to his over-stuffed high-back chair, but there was no question he was still alert and energetic.

"Well, Henry," he started. "I've already been briefed concerning your performance here at the stadium and I've been told that you worked out fairly well with us the past few days. How do you feel, son?" he asked. "Do you think you had a good workout?"

I didn't hesitate in giving him an answer to what I felt was nothing more than one of his standard ice-breaking interview questions. "Yes, sir, Mr. Rickey," I replied. "I think I was given a pretty good workout and I sure gave it my best shot."

There was a quiet pause before he continued as he seemed to be calculating the direction he wanted this discussion to take. I was taking so much of his small talk as just formality.

"Well, that's what we want to see out of everyone in this organization," he continued. "We want nothing less than everyone's best effort." At this point the tone of his voice suddenly became more business like. "Now, Henry, the scouting reports I received from Mr. Bowen and Coach Sukeforth were all positive and that's what I like to see." Again, there was a short pause as he pondered his next words. "Now just where is it you're from, son?" he inquired, pretending to be uninformed.

"Norfolk, sir, Norfolk, Virginia" I answered respectfully.

"Well, Henry, as I recall, that's the same area where that boy is from who just signed with the Red Sox for all that money. Isn't that right? And what's that young man's name?"

"Yes, sir, Mr. Rickey, that's right. His name is Chuck Stobbs, he's a left-handed pitcher and Chuck was a classmate of mine back at Granby High School."

With no obvious consideration for my answer, he seemed to let it slip by. Daddy, who had been silent to this point, turned his attention away from Mr. Rickey and stared at me with a serious yet thoughtful look on his face. We were both beginning to realize where his questions were leading us.

"Well, I don't guess I can talk with you since he got all that money," he concluded. After such a negative remark from the old man, my father leaned forward in his chair and reached for his hat.

"Okay, son," he spoke up, "if he can't talk with us, then let's go. There's no need for us to stay around here."

The cigar stub almost fell from the old man's lips as we both stood up and headed for the door. He may have had more to say, but we didn't stick around to find out. An abrupt halt in our negotiation talks was certainly not what Daddy and I had planned, nor was it what Mr. Rickey had expected. But, like my father pointed out to me moments later in the elevator, "Business is business, son, and we'll be hearing from him again sometime soon."

Mr. Branch Rickey with his trademark stub of a cigar between his lips. I was suddenly taken by what were likely the thickest, bushiest eyebrows I had ever seen.

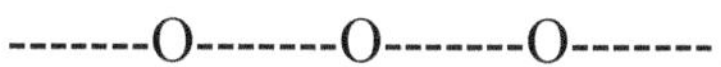

In 1976 the business of baseball changed drastically and forever. Prior to that time every professional baseball player who entered into a contractual agreement was legally bound to his team by what was known as the reserve clause. With this clause, the control and rights to each player was held solely by the club. A player was nothing more than the property of the team until he was sold, traded or until he quit or retired and was no longer an active player. It was the terms under which all players from my era, and all that had come before, were forced to play. Yet, it was legally applied to no other business in America except for baseball. As unfair as it may have been, this was the law of the land in pro baseball, until Americans were set to celebrate our nation's 200th birthday and the era of free agency began.

Years ago, there was another dubious baseball law on the books that greatly influenced the contract terms of many of the best young players throughout the country. It was referred to as baseball's bonus rule. The purpose of this controversial standard was to prevent the wealthier teams from signing all of the best prospects to lucrative contracts and locking them up for safe keeping in the minor leagues. It first went into effect soon after the end of World War II, and it required the club to place any first-year player who signed for an annual salary of more than $6,000 on its major league roster. At this point the club could exercise only one option on the contract. This meant the team could send that player to the minor leagues only once, for a period not to exceed one season. These "bonus babies" and the stipulations of their agreements would sometimes curtail a team's personnel moves and restrict the assignment of major league veterans. Because the rule reserved a roster spot for any bonus baby for two calendar years, the result was one less spot on the parent team, which could otherwise be filled by an experienced major leaguer. After he signed for a big five-figure bonus with the Red Sox, it was this rule that assured my former high school teammate, Chuck Stobbs, of a big league spot in Boston for his first two professional seasons. And as my father and I had already witnessed firsthand, it was this crazy bonus rule, which was finally disposed of in the mid-60s that drove certain team executives like Branch Rickey absolutely mad.

We were back home in Norfolk, fresh from our Brooklyn trip when I learned of another offer to travel. There was hardly time enough for Daddy and me to unpack our suitcases before my mother handed me a letter which had arrived just a day or so earlier. The envelope was marked with the unmistakable red, white and blue Yankee logo and the papers inside were nothing less than the passport to a young man's dreams. It was an invitation for me to travel with the New York Yankees on a western road trip! They asked that I accompany their major league team to four American League cities on what was called a western road swing. The letter went on to explain that I would benefit from the experience of life on the road with the team and about the advantages I would gain working out each day with major league players. Of course, the entire trip was by train and included hotel accommodations for each city, beginning with a short two-game visit in Detroit, followed by three games in Cleveland and leading on to stopovers for more games in Chicago and St. Louis before returning home to New York.

There would be no need to convince me, no further persuasion was necessary. I would have to have been crazy to even question such an opportunity as this one. The Yankee team was stocked with some of the biggest stars in baseball and had been holding onto first place in the American League since the middle of June. With just a little more than a month left in the season, they are sure to be going to the World Series. Getting this offer was the thrill of a lifetime and I would have been ready to go the next day if that's what they had wanted!

Needless to say, for nine days in August 1947, I was living a dream. Whether it was on the train, in the hotel, the dinning room or at the ballpark, each day I was in the company of many of the New York Yankees' all-time greats, including Joe DiMaggio, Phil Rizzuto, Yogi Berra and the "Superchief," Allie Reynolds. My roommate, Billy Johnson, the starting third baseman was a great guy. He had just returned to the team a year earlier, having lost two years from the prime of his career because of wartime military service. Yet, Billy had been around long enough to know the Yankees' routine and he made certain I was never left on my own at any time during the trip.

There was never much doubt that this club would go on to become World Champions that year and would be recognized as one of the greatest teams in Yankee history. They captured the A.L. pennant by a twelve-game margin and edged out Jackie Robinson and the Brooklyn Dodgers in a down-to-the-wire, seven-game World Series.

After my Yankee excursion, I had a difficult time getting my feet back on the ground and my head out of the clouds. The news of my trip created quite a clamor around the neighborhood, making headlines in the local sports section and drawing lots of attention from the folks around town. I even heard from a number of "old friends" that I didn't know I had. However, it was at the peak of this hubbub that my situation became even more complex.

Just as my father had predicted, the Dodgers had not abandoned the hunt. If anything, they had become even more determined to secure my signature as Mr. Rickey had Rex

Bowen drop by the house for another visit. This time Rex brought along an eye-popping contract offer which included a $35,000 signing bonus! While Daddy had assured me that we would be hearing more from the Dodgers, the staggering numbers of this proposal were a lot more than either of us had expected. Just the idea of having the first place teams of both the American and National Leagues vying for my services was too much for me to handle alone. At that point in my life, I may have thought of myself as a mature adult, a grown man in many ways. But at eighteen years old, I was never more grateful for the advice and level-headed reasoning of my father.

With his experience and incredible insight into the game, Daddy was able to point out to me a basic misconception that is often formed by many who are considered baseball experts. His thinking was centered on the expectations placed on young pitchers and catchers about to turn professional. And in keeping with what was his way of allowing me the freedom to make my own choices, his recommendations were always given to me as advice, he was never demanding.

"The deal Chuck Stobbs got from the Red Sox may work out okay. He signed for a big bonus and he'll have a place on the big club in Boston for two years. But keep in mind, he's a pitcher," he cautioned. "As a pitcher, Chuck might be able to learn his job well enough in that time to justify keeping him in the big leagues, but you're a catcher, son. Your work is a lot different. There's a lot more for a young catcher to learn before earning a job in the majors," he advised. "That might be too much to expect in just two seasons."

There was no question that the Dodgers' offer was tempting. I could plan to use the bonus money in ways that would benefit both me and my family but still, there were other things to consider. I needed to be mindful of my father's advice and look further into my future than just the next two years. No doubt, agreeing to sign with Brooklyn as a bonus baby would have been a lucrative deal. Yet, I couldn't see being content as a young catcher with limited playing time, who takes up the roster spot of a more experienced player.

The Yankees, on the other hand, were still anxious to further our talks. Again, they had my dad and me meet with them at their business offices in New York. Members of the club's top brass were assembled there, giving us an impression as to the importance of the meeting. Newly appointed general manager, George Weiss along with his legendary chief scout, Paul Krichell, were there. Krichell, an elderly bespectacled gentleman, had worked as a scout since 1920 and is best remembered for signing such Yankee greats as Lou Gehrig, Red Rolfe, Phil Rizzuto and Vic Raschi. With Mr. Krichell in attendance that day, I could only hope that I would become another in his long list of success stories. Also, making a trip up from Virginia was my father's trusted friend, Percy Dawson, who had left behind the busy operations of the Norfolk Tars and found his way clear to be with us.

The mindset that my father and I carried into this meeting was to simply ask for what was fair for both sides. We only insisted on arriving at a salary that was competitive and reasonable, considering my other available offer. After just a few minutes of discussion, the terms of a suitable contract were reached by the five of us, there in George Weiss's office. As was typical of the time, there were no lawyers or agents present that afternoon. Ours was a verbal agreement, solidified and finalized by a handshake, which was sufficient for my father and me. For us it was all a matter of trust, with no thoughts at all about who in the room would go back on his word. Besides, my father instilled in me at a very young age, that a man is as good as his word and his handshake is as good as his bond.

The terms we agreed upon called for me to be paid a salary of $6,000 a year for my first three years, commencing with the following baseball season in 1948. As a special provision, which would help with my taxes, it was agreed that I would receive $3,000, or half of the first year's money during 1947, even though it was too late in the season to have me start playing. I was set to earn the balance during the following year.

My professional career got underway on schedule in the spring of 1948, when the Yankees assigned me to their class B team of the New England League in Manchester, New Hampshire. Under the direction of our skipper, Tom Padden himself, a former big league catcher, our club managed only a mediocre season. I must admit that I did little to help the cause, finishing with offensive numbers that were less than impressive. It was a long and tiring season as Padden had me working behind the plate almost everyday. Yet, that season served as my introduction to the "bus leagues." It would be my first of several such minor league campaigns, where I seemed to have spent entire summers riding in a hot, over-packed, rickety old bus, traveling from one tiny town to the next. However, it was a disappointing situation which unfolded after my season in Manchester that changed my view of baseball management forever.

It wasn't until the days leading up to spring training in 1949, when I received my contract for the upcoming season, that I learned the hard way about the lack of integrity on the part of my employers. Instead of sending me a contract for $6,000 as agreed, my contract was for only $3,000! At first Daddy concluded that there must be a misunderstanding. He contacted the Yankees, hoping to solve the discrepancy in a civil way. He tried to remind them of the terms of our agreement, only to be told in no uncertain terms, there was no mistake; the salary would remain at $3,000, the same as the year before….take it or leave it! This was still the era of the reserve clause, so naturally we had no recourse; the control of my contract fell completely with the ball club. My father, with nowhere left to turn, felt terribly responsible for us being setup for such an underhanded swindle. Moreover, at eighteen years old, I was still considered a minor, which dictated that my contract carry his signature as well as mine, making us both victims of this deceitful double-cross.

Daddy was as angry and disgusted as I had ever known him to be. He wanted nothing more than for me to be treated fairly and to be given a fresh start. By no means was he a wealthy man, yet he was able to find a way to scrape together enough money to buy back my contract from the Yankees, only to be refused. With only one card left to play, he called on his longtime friend, Percy Dawson.

"Percy, you and I have been friends for a long time," my father began. "You were in our meeting in New York. You know what my son was promised just as well as I know what he was promised. You know he was cheated out of *three thousand dollars*. Now Percy, I want you to speak up for what's right. I need you to go to bat for us."

At first my dad got no response. Finally after a deep sigh, Percy looked Daddy right in the eye and proceeded to expose his own shortage of moral character.

"I'd like to do that, Henry," he pleaded. "I know what the terms of the deal were. But, if I did something like that, I would lose my job with the Yankees."

With those words the book was closed on a long-standing friendship. After that short conversation, my father and Percy Dawson never spoke to one another again. Our dealings with the Yankees proved to be a bitter, yet valuable lesson to learn, but, maybe it was best that I found out early in my career the harsh realities that existed in the business of professional baseball.

Joe L. Brown was a baseball executive who was a man of his word.

It wasn't until years later when I was with the Pittsburgh Pirates that I encountered a baseball executive who proved to be an individual of true character and a man of his word. This gentleman was Joe L. Brown, the team's legendary general manager. I found him to be trustworthy in his business agreements and fair to players on the club, as long as they were giving their best efforts. Joe even came through with a fairly hefty pay raise when I confronted him about my good performance and my meager salary. "You didn't hit like you should have," he countered. "You didn't have that good of a year."

I called his attention to the number of games I had caught that season while dealing with the pain of a couple of cracked fingers, which hampered my grip on the bat. "I was in there everyday, Joe," I reminded him. "I just couldn't get a good swing with that busted hand." He must have considered my side of the story when the time came to renew my contract. I was pleased to find that the salary increase he offered was very rewarding.

My dealings with Dawson, Weiss and the other Yankees would not be my last involvement with unscrupulous characters in the game. Over the years I would conclude that there are individuals of this type employed by every team in both leagues. However, this was not just *any* team. This was the New York Yankees, the one organization recognized for decades as the single most successful sports operation in history.

So, as parting advice for those who have not yet learned, you must remember….

Not all that glitters is gold!

Baseball

Ford C. Frick
Commissioner
Charles M. Segar
Secretary-Treasurer

RCA Building, West
30 Rockefeller Plaza
New York 20, N. Y.

October 21, 1952

Mr. Henry L. Foiles, Jr.
1419 Morris Crescent
Norfolk 5, Virginia

My dear Mr. Foiles:

Again I acknowledge your telegram of October 14th, in which you make a claim for certain salary and apply for your free agency.

As I wired you, this matter has been taken up with the Cincinnati and the Ottawa Clubs. I am now in receipt of a wire from Elmer Burkhart, of the Ottawa Club, which says: "Due to error in our books Foiles did not receive balance of his 1952 salary. Check in the amount of $450.00 has been forwarded to Foiles. Sorry to cause you this inconvenience".

Receipt of this check, of course, constitutes full payment of the salary due you. In your claim for free agency you report, "a period of 43 days has elapsed since I was last paid. I notified the Cincinnati Club October 6, 1952 that my salary was in arrears". The 43 days cannot be taken as an accurate statement. At least 15 days of that must elapse before any payment was due. Your case was referred by you to me on October 14th. Check in payment of the back salary was forwarded you immediately and at no time was there any effort on the part of either club to avoid payment of this salary. It was simply a question of which club was obligated to make the payment.

Under the circumstances, your appeal for free agency is denied.

Sincerely

Ford Frick

FF/ms

Case in point, I would not be paid until a determination was made by Baseball Commissioner Ford Frick, which ball club was responsible for paying my salary.

CHAPTER 10

MY NAME IS JOE!

Ask any of us senior citizens to recall our most memorable events of 1948 and the responses you get will likely be as varied as patterns for a snow flake. Considering that the year marked the start of our country's post-war economic boom, some may say it was the year they purchased their first home or their first new automobile. Many may quickly bring up that it was the year our country first acknowledged the newly-formed Jewish State of Israel. Still others will chuckle as they draw on old memories of that year's presidential election and the erroneous newspaper headlines which prematurely declared, *DEWEY DEFEATS TRUMAN!*

But from me, you won't get any of the top answers which are likely to show up in a public survey of American old-timers. For me, it was the year I would turn 19 years old and when compared to most other young men fresh out of high school, I was a little off the norm. I had baseball on the brain! My biggest and fondest recollection of that year was spring training, as it was my first and by far, my most exciting and memorable.

I got my first taste of professional baseball in February 1948 when I reported to the Yankees' spring training camp in St. Petersburg, Florida. As you can imagine, it was a daunting experience for me to walk into the old clubhouse at Miller Huggins Field for the first time and find myself in the company of so many of my baseball idols. There were Bill

Dickey, Joe DiMaggio, Charlie Keller, Yogi Berra, Billy Johnson, Phil Rizzuto and so many other famous Yankee stars, all gathered in one place. For one of the first times in my life I was truly frightened and intimidated. After not being together over the winter, these veteran players had a lot of catching up to do. It was time for them to renew their friendships and get started on another season together. They were boisterous and loud, laughing, shaking hands, greeting each other like brothers at a family reunion. All the while I was quiet, trying hard to hide my fears. I couldn't let any of them see that my hands were shaking or that my knees were quivering. I suddenly became aware of what it was like to go from being a big fish in a small pond to nothing more than a tiny minnow in a big ocean of talent!

I was finally able to breathe a little more easily when I spotted two other young fellows standing near the door who seemed to be just as nervous and out of place as I was. After some quick introductions, I found that the three of us were the only rookies who had been invited to the Yankees' big league camp. One of these hopefuls was Clarence "Clarky" Wojtowicz, a tall, athletically-built outfielder from Chicopee, Massachusetts. He would go on to play several more years in the Yankee chain, but would never get a shot at playing in the major leagues. And despite being heralded "the next Joe DiMaggio," Pete Gentile, the second of the pair, was another strong, well-built outfielder who would be destined to play out his career in the minors.

One of the first things we learned that first day in the clubhouse was the well defined boundaries of the team's pecking order. While each of the veteran players had his own dressing area, complete with a spacious locker and a tall dressing stool, the trio of us newcomers was assigned "lockers" which were nothing more than a few nails driven into the side of a thick partition. And while this bulky partition, with its makeshift coat hooks, served as a place for us to hang our street clothes, it also worked as a barrier, one which helped keep us out of the way and isolated from the rest of the team.

One of my first duties as a Yankee farmhand was to get out to the field by 8 o'clock each morning and catch batting practice for any of the regulars who wanted to get started early. This group of early-bird hitters, who wanted to get in some extra work before the rest of the squad arrived, included the club's starting outfielders Joe DiMaggio, John Lindell and Tommy Henrich.

In addition to this bunch of heavy hitters, the Yankee's spring roster also carried a number of experienced catchers, all well seasoned and very capable. Yet as they came out of the clubhouse with the rest of the team, guys like Yogi Berra, Charlie Silvera and Aaron Robinson could have easily stepped in as the batting practice catcher and bumped me out of a job. But apparently my spot was not a job in high demand. Now for what seemed like an endless stream of batters, I stayed behind the plate, laboring for what must have been a period of three hours or more, not to mention how sitting on my haunches that long can make for a long day. Finally, a young, hard-nosed catcher named Ralph Houk, just up from an impressive year in the minors, stepped to the plate wearing his catcher's gear and offered to take over for me. Of course, most baseball fans will remember how Ralph moved on to a great career as a successful manager for the Yankees and a couple of other American League clubs. But, I'll always remember him for his thoughtful gesture on that bright chilly day when he gave me a much needed break from catching, during a tiresome workout at my first spring training.

In order to be on time for early batting practice, I made it a point to rise early and be the first to arrive at the clubhouse each morning. Our hotel was at least two, maybe three miles from Huggins Field, so after a good breakfast I would get started on my walk to the clubhouse which was a good physical workout in itself. I would then retrace my steps for a long walk back to my room each afternoon. I deliberately kept to myself and had very little to say to anyone during my first few weeks in the Yankees' training camp. I felt about as uneasy as a canary at a cat show!

After a full day of workouts and drills, the clubhouse was quiet and almost empty when I finished my shower and got dressed. Just about everyone had already left for the day, so I figured it was time for me to make my way back to the hotel. As I came walking from behind the big partition and headed for the front area of the locker room, I suddenly and unexpectedly walked up on the great Joe DiMaggio. He was sitting at his locker, stripped down to his long-sleeve undershirt, his knee length under-shorts and his stirrups and sanitary socks. He was sitting alone, relaxing with a Camel cigarette and his typical half cup of coffee. (To my knowledge, Joe always preferred to be served only a half cup of coffee. He complained that a full cup of coffee would get cold before he could finish it.) He looked up at me from his chair and blew a cloud of smoke towards the ceiling. He spoke to me as if he were waiting to have a word with the next person to pass by.

"What do you do around here?" he asked.

"Well, I think I'm a catcher, Mr. DiMaggio," I stuttered nervously. "I've been catching batting practice for you every morning at 8 o'clock for the past three weeks."

"Well, son, you know I can't ever tell who's behind the plate wearing all of that catcher's gear," he conceded. "But thanks, you've been doing a fine job."

Without giving me a chance to say "you're welcome," he went on talking. "I want to ask you something," he continued, "where are you going now?"

I was trying hard to keep my composure, while being careful to be respectful.

"I'm just heading back over to the hotel, Mr. DiMaggio," I replied.

Joe couldn't tell who it was behind the plate wearing all of that catcher's gear.

He wasted no time in getting to his next question. "Tell me this," he pried, "can you throw strikes?"

At this point I couldn't imagine what he could want from me, but I figured it would be best if I made myself available and gave him an affirmative response.

"Yes sir, Mr. DiMaggio," I piped up, "I can throw strikes."

"Well, that's great, son," he said, pleased by my answer. "Well, how about pitching some batting practice to me?"

"Sure, Mr. DiMaggio," I replied without a second thought.

"And by the way, my name is Joe," he assured me. "Just call me Joe."

"Yes sir, Mr. DiMaggio!" I answered eagerly, unable to drop my respect. "I'm sorry about that, Mr. DiMaggio, but that's just the way my parents raised me, it's just how I was brought up."

I hurried back behind the partition and grabbed my uniform, pulling it down from the nails. I had never been as nervous and excited as I was then, forcing the buttons through the holes of that old pinstriped flannel shirt. But somehow, with shaky fingers, I managed to get my buttons buttoned and my shoes tied and in minutes I was out of the locker room and on the mound, pitching batting practice to my new friend, Joe DiMaggio!

I was thankful that my nerves didn't prevent me from delivering strikes and that Joe was able to connect with just about every ball I threw to him. With the help of Yankees' longtime clubhouse manager, "Big" Pete Sheehy and his assistant, "Little" Pete Previte, shagging and retrieving balls in the outfield, our practice session went as smooth as silk. Joe seemed satisfied with the workout and after about 20 or 25 minutes, he decided to call it a day. We headed back to the locker room for showers, my second one within the hour.

I was dressed and preparing to leave the clubhouse for a second time when I found Joe again, at his locker enjoying another Camel and a half cup of coffee.

"So, what do you have planned for tonight?" he asked, as I walked up.

"Well, not a whole lot, Mr. DiMaggio. I just thought I'd go back to the hotel and get some dinner and maybe take in a movie. I really don't have much planned," I admitted.

"Well, do you like Italian food?" he asked. "You see, I have some friends who own a nice little Italian restaurant over at Pass-A-Grille Beach, and I'm about to drive out there for dinner. Would you like to join me?"

"Yes, sir," I answered without hesitation. "Sure, I love Italian food."

"Okay, son, it's all set. You're going out with *the Big Dago* tonight!"

Together we walked outside to the players' parking lot and jumped into Joe's new '48 Cadillac. Heading straight towards a beautiful sunset on the Gulf of Mexico, Joe drove from Huggins Field, west for about thirty minutes to the tiny town of Pass-A-Grille, a small resort community lying on the coastal outskirts of St. Petersburg. The restaurant he selected was delightful. As we passed from the front entrance and through the dining area the wonderful aroma of Italian cuisine told me that Joe really knew how to pick a good place to eat.

He introduced me to his friends, the owners, a lovely couple who escorted us to a special secluded table reserved just for Joe. It was his request to be seated away from the regular dining room, so he wouldn't be recognized or disturbed by the public during dinner. We relaxed and enjoyed the evening at his private table, overlooking the beautiful waters of the Gulf and feasting on some of the finest Italian dishes money could buy.

"Hank," he asked, "do your parents allow you to have a beer?"

"Yes, sir, they do," I replied, finishing a sip of my ice water

"Okay, here's the deal," he said in a parental tone. "Tonight you can have one beer and one glass of red wine with your meal, but that's the limit for tonight."

"Yes, sir, Mr. DiMaggio," I agreed, "whatever you say."

He looked down at his plate and slowly nodded his head in frustration. "Joe!" he reminded me one last time. "My name is Joe!"

For the remaining weeks of training camp, Joe took me under his wing. He not only became a good friend, but in some ways he treated me like his own son. After our first dinner together, he invited me on other occasions to go with him to the dog tracks and to join him for dinner at other restaurants. Joe was a wise, yet quiet and private person. Some may even say he was aloof and snobbish. Yet at a time when he was at the height of his career, I found him to be a kind, caring and generous individual who did everything necessary to make an 18-year-old rookie feel confident and special.

In many of our conversations he offered advice which would help me not only with my baseball career, but with life in general. He told me of the importance of having confidence and to never doubt my own abilities.

"When you find yourself in a tight spot," he advised, "and the game is on the line, always remember, your opponent put his pants on the same way you did....one leg at a time!"

Thanks for everything, Joe. I'll never forget you.

After entering the game as a pinch runner for Joe DiMaggio, I came in to score in exhibition play against the Phillies at Al Lang Field in St. Petersburg, Florida.

CHAPTER 11

THE BUS LEAGUES

As far back as the 1920s when Branch Rickey first used lower level professional teams to cultivate players for the big leagues, there have been many different ways to refer to baseball's system of player development. And now that most cities across America big enough to have an airport and a hospital also have their own pro baseball team, everyone is familiar with the most frequently used term, minor leagues. But other names like bush leagues, farm leagues, instructional and developmental leagues are all used to describe basically the same thing. However, when a discussion turns to any part of my professional career other than the majors, I always talk about my seasons in the *Bus Leagues.*

For too many years and too many miles, I endured trips on hot over-crowded buses all over the country, rolling through the back roads and freeways from one small town to the next. It was a simple fact of life, a rite of passage for any player who ever hoped to reach the top. And as any major leaguer from my era will tell you, it caused us to have a deep appreciation for the more luxurious life in baseball once we finally made it.

Because of bonuses, higher salaries, and special contract provisions some of today's rising stars will never experience life in the bus leagues as I knew it. Many of today's top draft choices will never know what it is like to ride an old worn out Greyhound which had seen its best miles many years before. Sometimes held together by nothing more than some wire and a few pieces of duct tape, these buses offered little more than the comfort of a horse and wagon. It was nearly impossible to get comfortable and for most of us sleep was out of the question. Many players who had given up on the hopes of falling asleep would get involved in a card game instead. Four-handed pinochle, the game of choice, was usually in full swing in the rear of the bus where a firm sheet of cardboard served adequately as a portable card table. With two players seated on the wide rear seat and two more seated on the aisle seats of the next row, a noisy card game would often last all night. Strangely enough, that special piece of cardboard received as much care and attention as any other piece of vital team equipment when the time came to pack up for a road trip.

My first experiences in the bus leagues were far from ordinary. That first spring training with the New York Yankees in 1948 was the thrill of a lifetime, but when camp broke and the team headed north to start the season, I didn't have a clue as to where my next assignment would take me, and it was obvious that the ball club wasn't quite sure what to do with me either. I knew from the beginning that I wouldn't make the big team at the start of the regular season since they had such a backlog of talent and experience at the catcher position. But being in training camp with so many of my boyhood idols sure was exciting.

When the Yankees left camp in St. Petersburg and headed north, I was handed a bus ticket and told to head east. After about two or three hours of dozing and staring out of the window at the flat lands of central Florida, I got off at the Greyhound terminal in Lake Wales. A small town located in Polk County, Lake Wales was the spring training home of the Yankees' Triple-A farm team, the Kansas City Blues, and it would be my baseball home for the next couple of weeks.

There, too, I didn't expect to remain with the team for the beginning of the season as this club had just come off a stellar season in 1947. The Blues had captured the American Association championship with a strong offensive team featuring future Yankee stars Hank Bauer, Jerry Coleman and Tommy Byrne and was still loaded with good catchers, having Ralph Houk and Charlie Silvera in camp. Nevertheless, the team's new manager, Dick Bartell, a former National League all-star shortstop, kept me busy working out daily with hitting and defensive drills. By the time the Blues' spring camp ended I was in tremendous physical shape and ready to start the season. Yet I still didn't know what sort of plans the Yankees had for me.

Finally, when everyone else was packing and preparing to break camp, I was called into Bartell's office and presented with another bus ticket. This time it was for what would be only the first of the really long bus rides that I would take during my minor league career. I was bound for Edenton, North Carolina, to participate in my third training camp of the spring.

The long tiring journey, which took almost 14 hours, finally ended outside of a bus station in the downtown section of Edenton and by the time I finally stepped off the bus, carrying my bags and gear, I was quite hungry. But like all of the other players on the team, I was restricted to just one place to eat in the entire town. The ball club had an arrangement with a small lunch counter located inside of a gas station, no less, where we were allowed to pick our breakfast and dinner from three or four of the cheapest items on the menu. Just about all of us ate there twice a day while we were in town for training camp, signing our receipts after each meal, so the club could pick up the tab. As stingy as they were, the Yankees wouldn't cover our lunches at the diner. Our lunches, if you could call them that, consisted of a sandwich and a carton of milk, provided for us in the clubhouse, which, as you can imagine, wasn't a very appetizing place to eat. Sure, I was a little weary from the long ride, but I was only 18 years old and had not yet learned the true meaning of the word "tired." So as soon as I could scarf down a sandwich and a Coke, I'd be good to go, ready to play baseball the rest of the day.

This training camp, located near the banks of the Albemarle Sound in northeastern North Carolina, had just opened for the year and was occupied by Yankee farmhands who had already survived a year or two of professional play. It was the Manchester Yankees of the class B New England League, and our manager there, Tommy Padden, a former big league catcher, was in complete charge. He was a remarkable fellow with a lot of baseball under his belt and a genuine love for the game. You would think that at this point in his life he would have had his fill of bus trips and cocky young boys who each thought he was the best player ever. Yet, Tommy continued to work for the Yankees, first as a minor league coach and instructor and then as manager at Manchester. He had more than his hands full on this job, having to oversee about two dozen hopeful prospects, including some who were barely old enough to shave.

Padden took one look at me and commented on my deep sun tan. "My gosh, Foiles," he barked. "How long did they keep you down there in Florida--six months?" He was aware that I had already been in camp for a full spring with the big club and was then sent out to train with the Kansas City Blues in Lake Wales. "We need to give you a break," he decided. "We need to give you some time off, because you are already way ahead of these boys who are just getting started. I want you to go home for about a week, take it easy for a while and then come back and join us for the rest of the spring. I just don't want you getting too fine."

Tom Padden (right), my manager at Manchester, had a lot of baseball under his belt and a genuine love of the game.

His orders sounded like a great idea to me. I was ready for some time at home as I knew this would be my only chance to get away from baseball until the season was finished. *This would work out just right. I'm only a couple of hours from home, so only a small part of my time would be spent traveling. Besides, a bus ticket back to Norfolk and a chance to be with my lovely fiancée, Joyce, would be exactly what I need.* The reception I received when I got home was not.

"What in the world are you doing here?" my daddy demanded to know. I had just walked through the front door when his questions started. "Did you leave the team? You're supposed to be playing baseball. Have you been released, did they cut you?" It took a moment before he quieted down enough for me to get a word in. This kind of reaction was not what I had expected.

"They gave me some time off, Daddy," I explained. "They wanted me leave camp for a few days while the other players work into shape. Tommy Padden said I was too far ahead of the others. These fellows are just getting started and I've been training since the middle of February."

Daddy's position was not swayed by any of this. "Well we'll see about this!" he snapped. "All I know is that you're a ball player and you're supposed to be in spring training. So bright and early tomorrow morning we'll be on our way. I'm driving you back to Edenton, to training camp where you belong!"

I wasn't about to argue. I simply resolved myself to make the most of my brief time at home. I was delighted to see Joyce, the love of my life, and happy to get a chance to have some of Momma's home cooking. I even squeezed in a good night's sleep in my own bed. But you can bet I was packed and ready to jump into the car with Daddy the following morning for an early ride to North Carolina.

Throughout the entire trip he constantly harped about how leaving the team could do nothing but lessen my standing with the team and he didn't care to hear anything to the contrary. I was smart enough to know when to keep quiet.

"Where did you come from?" Padden demanded to know when I walked into the clubhouse. "You don't belong here! Didn't you understand what I told you? You're supposed to be at home, relaxing and enjoying yourself."

"Yes, sir, I fully understand. But it's my dad, he didn't like the idea of me being at home and he drove me all the way back down here this morning. So you'll have to take this matter up with him."

"It makes no difference about your dad!" he declared. I want you at home. Like I told you before, Hank, you're way out in front of these fellows here, so go home and come back in a week."

Daddy had no choice but to accept the orders of my manager. I'm sure he had nothing but the best intentions and wasn't about to allow anything to happen that would derail my chances and his hopes for my success. Perhaps he wanted me to reach the levels of play he never experienced. Maybe he was living his dreams through me. Either way, the situation made for a long quiet ride back to Norfolk. And wouldn't you know it, Momma had supper waiting for us when we rolled into the driveway.

Once our spring training was completed in North Carolina, we were in for what perhaps would be the longest bus ride any of us would ever take. Our journey along the Atlantic Coast would take almost 16 hours and would carry us about 800 miles northward to New Hampshire. It was there at Manchester's Municipal Athletic Field where I played my first professional baseball game. I took the field along with teammates, Ray Schmidt, a right-handed pitcher, and shortstop Frank Verdi, fellows who would prove to be two of the best friends I would ever make in baseball. Incidentally, the two-man umpiring crew assigned to work my first game consisted of Frank Umont and Hank Soar, a couple of former New York Giant football stars who would go on to have great careers as umpires in the American League. As the twists and turns of life evolved I would encounter these two fellows quite often when I too was in the A.L. I will have to say for the pair, that I always appreciated their dedication and integrity and I will list the two of them among the best umpires who ever called a game.

But don't get the idea that long bus rides were all there was to life in the minor leagues. Finding good places to eat and a good place to stay when the team was at home were priorities as well. It was while on a road trip that summer that pizza became a mainstay of my diet. I believe it was in Springfield or maybe Pawtucket that some of the guys found a small Italian restaurant that featured some great prices on their menu. It was just the type of joint we needed to find as we all struggled to stay within our three-buck-a-day food allotment. It was there that we could buy a huge pizza, which was at least 30 inches in diameter, for $2.00, plus a large-sized mug of beer for a nickel. This was enough to satisfy four of us at a cost of just 55 cents each! I don't seem to recall just how generous we were when it came to leaving a tip, but I am sure that we never left that place hungry.

As for finding a place to live that season, I hit the jackpot when I first met Mr. and Mrs. Gallagher, a very friendly elderly couple who lived there in Manchester. These folks owned a large old two-story house with upstairs rooms to let. Ray Schmidt and I each rented rooms in their home for the summer. This gave us the best living arrangements and accommodations we could ever want. The entire second floor was ours and we each had our own private bedroom while we shared a spacious livingroom and a full bathroom. Ray, who was one of the older players on the club, was a great roommate who also had his own car adding to our easy convenient lifestyle. Our landlords who treated us like family were wonderful people. Later during the season my parents met the Gallaghers when they drove up from Virginia to watch me play a few games. All concerns that my mother may have had about my life away from home were quickly put to rest. One visit with the Gallaghers and a walk up to second floor to see my room was all it took to win her over and assure both Momma and Daddy that I was living with some fine people.

One of my most unfortunate incidents while playing in the minors occurred while my parents were visiting in Manchester. We were playing a home game under the lights with the Nashua Dodgers when I went to bat against Dan Bankhead, a tall right-hander with a lively fastball.

Bankhead, who was known for his wildness, had seen action a year earlier with Brooklyn when he moved up to the parent club to become the first black pitcher in the major leagues. Maybe it was the insufficient lighting or maybe I was just slow to react, but it was a Bankhead fastball that struck me in my forehead, in a spot right between my eyes. I went down at the plate as if I had been shot with a gun. I lay there unconscious for a minute or so. Of course I didn't witness any of this, but from the reports I heard from Frank Verdi and some other players, my father became involved in the scary scene the very second I was hit. The accounts I got later claimed that he jumped from his place along the first few rows and leaped upwards towards the dugout. He jumped completely over the wall in front of the seats, cleared the dugout and flew high over the protective railing in front of the players' bench. He finally landed on the field, well out into foul territory. In one swift move, he popped up and immediately tore out for homeplate. There would be no stopping him from getting to me.

I was taken from the field to the clubhouse where, lying on the trainer's table, I started to regain my senses. "You're through for tonight," I heard Padden say with his words echoing in my head.

I tried to look up from the table and regain my vision. I cleared my head and slowly recognized the fuzzy, blurry outline of Daddy's face. "He'll be okay!" he reassured my manager. "Put him back out there tomorrow night and he'll be fine." I knew from a young age that it was my father's firm belief "if you fell off a horse, the best thing to do is get right back on!" He was there to make sure his theory was put to the test.

I realized that Dad's primary concern was not so much about my consciousness or my physical well being. No way! He was convinced my injury was not a serious one and that was not his way. His big concern was whether I would be "gun shy" after being beaned and whether I would be mentally ready to get back up to bat and stand in there against another inside pitch. That was his unique way of caring. I'm sure his flying leap from the stands to the ball field was the topic of barber shop discussions around Manchester for many years to follow. It must have been a crazy scene.

I noticed no lingering effects from the beaning and had no other excuses for finishing the 1948 season with sub-par offensive numbers. I managed only four homers and batted a pinch over .230, but still at the end of the year I was voted the most popular player on the Manchester club, a recognition that made me more determined to work hard to be more productive next season.

In spite of my mediocre season in the New England League, I was promoted to the class A Binghamton Triplets for the '49 season. There, under the management of George Selkirk I teamed up with pitcher Whitey Ford, second sacker Loren Babe and third baseman Jim Greengrass, who were all top prospects in the Yankees' chain. Also there was my friend from the previous season in Manchester, infielder Frank Verdi.

With Selkirk, the veteran Yankee, best known for succeeding Babe Ruth in rightfield, as our skipper, I came through with a much better performance for the season, both defensively as well as hitting. I led our club with a .311 batting average which was good enough to place me in the top ten hitters of the Eastern League. However, with a record of 16-5 Whitey also had an outstanding campaign too, finishing among the top pitchers in the E.L. For that impressive effort, he was rewarded with a well-deserved promotion to New York at the start of the following year. But due to the overload of catching talent which still existed in the organization, I was held back and dispatched to Binghamton again in the spring of 1950 for another season.

Returning to the Triplets for another year didn't compare to drawing a promotion to New York, but at the same time, it wasn't the worst thing that could have happened to me. Our club had a pretty good season with pitcher Tom Morgan winning 17 ball games, while first baseman Dale Long knocked the cover off the ball, hitting for both power and average. Even my buddy from Brooklyn, New York, Frank Verdi, found a spot in the lineup everyday and batted over .300. For me, personally it was an exceptional year. My batting average of .333 was good enough to pace the team for the second straight season and to rank second among the league averages. I was lucky to edge out Phillies' prospect, Mel Clark of the Utica club by a single point, but ended up well behind top hitter, Hartford's George Crowe who finished at .353. Despite this list of positive notes the Triplets ended the season in second place, 9-1/2 games behind the Wilkes-Barre Indians. However, my big break of the year came about as the result of a foul tip and a fractured thumb in New York.

My new bride Joyce and I lived quietly and comfortably in our apartment in Binghamton and found the area to be to our liking for a number of reasons. We were close to the city's better restaurants and shopping spots and the moderate temperatures of New York were a lot more comfortable than the humid summer climate back home. But Joyce was ready to get out and explore that area of the country. She had never been to New York City and was anxious to see the Big Apple up close for herself.

As we approached mid-season, our schedule gave us a rare day off, which was the first one we had received since the start of spring training. As good luck would have it, it was a day with perfect weather, bright and sunny, just an ideal day for taking to the highway. My teammate, pitcher William "Red" Rose, a likeable fellow who lived nearby owned his own automobile and he too was ready to make the most of our day off and get out of town. Red and his wife suggested that Joyce and I ride along with them to New York and make it a full day of touring and sightseeing. Of course Joyce was all for the idea, so the four of us got an early morning start to make the round trip of over 400 miles. We would all enjoy the day, but it was all planned so she could see the subways, the unbelievable traffic and the skyscrapers for the first time. After a long but pleasurable day we arrived back in Binghamton just before dark only to find a big surprise waiting on our doorstep.

Joyce was ready to get out and explore that area of the country. She was anxious to see the Big Apple up close for herself.

It was Jim Cooper, the assistant GM and business manager of the Binghamton team, sitting and waiting for us to return. "Where have you guys been?" he asked, getting up from the steps and approaching the car. "I've been waiting for you for hours. Where have you been all day?"

"We've been to New York, Jim," I answered. "And I told George Selkirk all about it yesterday before we left. All you had to do was check with George to get your answers. So what's going on?" I insisted. "What's the big deal?"

"I'll tell you what's going on," he quipped, seeming a little agitated. "The Yankees have sent for you and they want you to meet them in Boston as soon as possible, that's the big deal!"

I didn't like to see Jim get upset, but as I explained to him, the lack of communication among team officials was no fault of mine. He appeared to calm down a little before he went into further details.

"They say Yogi Berra took a foul tip off his hand and the x-rays show that he has some broken bones. They want you to meet the club at Fenway Park right away and help out with the catching. Just get your stuff packed as quickly as you can and take along everything you'll need since they seem to have no idea how long you'll be with them." He then stared blankly into the distance for a few seconds as if he were overlooking something. "And oh yeah… there's one more thing. Here's your plane ticket to Boston. You'll need to get to the local airport here in Binghamton in a couple of hours to catch your flight and don't you dare miss it!"

"Thanks, Jim, I'll be on time," I said calmly as he turned away and headed for his car. "Don't worry about a thing. I'll be on time."

After a smooth flight and a taxi ride to the ballpark, I lugged my gear into the visitor's clubhouse at Fenway and the first person to greet me was trainer Gus Mauch. "What are you doing here, kid?" he asked in a surprised tone. "Are you lost?"

"No, Gus. They told me I was catching tonight. They said Yogi had a busted hand and they told me to get here as soon as I could. Where's my uniform?"

"Well, I don't know about all of that," he advised. "You'll have to see Casey when he gets back. Right now everyone is out on the field for batting practice, but he should be back in here any time now. I grabbed a seat in front of a vacant locker, but hardly had time to get comfortable before some of the players and coaches came walking through the tunnel doorway. Gus met Casey just inside the door, whispered a few words to him and pointed in my direction before leaving the room. Dressed in his Yankee road grays, Casey slowly waddled over to where I was sitting.

"What are you here for kid?" he asked, as if he were joking. "Are you here to see a ballgame?"

"No, sir," I answered quickly. "They told me I was catching tonight. I was told that Yogi had a bad thumb and you needed me to catch."

Standing nearby was Frank Scott, the club's traveling secretary who had just finished talking to me about some of the details about my flight from Binghamton. Casey turned to catch Frank's attention before he could slip away. "Scotty," he ordered, "take him on up to the stands. You fellows get a hotdog and a beer and watch the game!" In his own round-about way, Casey was letting me know that I wasn't about to do any catching.

I stayed with the Yankees for about three weeks and was never put into a game, but still I could think of no place I'd rather be. It was great to be assigned to the big club and traveling with many of my longtime idols was very exciting. Yet I remained anxious, still waiting to see my first action in the major leagues.

After stopping off in Philadelphia to square off with the Athletics, our next stop on the road trip was our nation's capital for a three-game series with the Senators. As in every other city where the Yankees play, the team was provided with the finest hotel and dining arrangements in the town. When staying in Washington, the Yankees' choice was always the Shoreham Hotel, a landmark luxury hotel located on Calvert Street in the northwest section of the district. The services and accommodations there exceeded anything I had experienced to this point in my short career and I had heard that eating in the hotel's dining room was a culinary event fit for a king. Some fellows on the club picked other places to eat in lieu of the Shoreham, as it was known to be too pricy for us, considering the stingy food allowance we received.

Not sure what to do or where to go for dinner, Hank Bauer and I were hanging out in the Shoreham lobby close to the entrance to the dining room. We were digging through our pockets to determine if we could afford to go in for just one meal. Our arithmetic proved that we would be cutting it close. "Damn, Hank!" Bauer exclaimed. "If we eat here tonight we won't have enough food money to last us the rest of the road trip. Maybe we should try another place," he suggested. I was about to agree with him when an unexpected friendly greeting came from behind us.

"Hey, fellows, what are you up to tonight?" It was Joe DiMaggio, dressed to the nines and smiling from ear to ear. He gave me a friendly pat on the back before he went to his next question. "Are you guys eating in here tonight?" he asked.

Bauer shoved both hands deep into the pockets of his trousers and looked at me with a wide-eyed expression that showed his nervous indecision. "Well, sure, Joe," he stuttered nervously. "Hank and I were just about to ..." He couldn't even complete his thought. That's when Joe cut in and made plans for all of three of us.

"Let's go on in here and get a table in The Garden," he proposed. "The Garden is always a little nicer than the dining room, so let's give that a try."

Now for all of us ballplayers, The Shoreham was noted as the crème de la crème, the best of all places to dine, but to have dinner in the elegant Shoreham Garden, that was taking it to a whole new level.

We had a memorable evening together, just the three of us, enjoying the superb dinner entrées and wine selections along with the pleasures of good conversation between friends. It was great to be with Joe again and to renew our relationship. We recalled some of the great experiences we shared in spring training over the past three years and it was great to find that he still had a special interest in me and my baseball career.

As our evening was about to come to a close, a uniformed waiter approached our table with a spotless white towel draped over his arm and our check in his hand, Bauer and I simultaneously reached for our wallets. We knew it was time to pay up. Both of us had been in baseball long enough to be familiar with the unwritten rule that states, "No matter how many guys are at the table and regardless of who ordered what, the bill will always be split evenly." So, Hank and I were ready to cover our share.

"No, no guys!" Joe alerted us when he noticed us fumbling for our money. "You don't need to do that, not tonight. It's on me. You're with t*he Big Dago* tonight!"

I paused in thought for a moment as I remembered hearing those same exact words a couple of years earlier, while in an Italian restaurant in Pass-a-Grille, Florida.

My goodness, it sure was great to be his friend!

The Binghamton Triplets of 1949, a club with an abundance of talent. That's me, third row, second from the left, standing behind my friend, Red Rose. Jim Cooper, Asst. GM is on back row, far right. Future Yankee great and Hall-of-Fame pitcher, Whitey Ford is on the second row, third from right.

My parents came to visit during my first season as a pro, in Manchester, NH in 1948.

CHAPTER 12

WE GET PAID TO UMPIRE, YOU DON'T!

In baseball there is no job as unappreciated and thankless as that of an umpire. Since the inception of the game, the notion among fans has been "the best umpire is the one who is never noticed." It takes a special person to be an umpire and for one to execute his duties flawlessly, while remaining practically invisible, calls for extraordinary talent. But like in any other profession, there are good umpires and bad ones. And while things like their skill levels, their degree of patience and their attitudes and personalities may vary, no one should ever question their passion for the game. Without unwavering dedication and love for baseball, none of these fellows would ever reach the pinnacle of their profession and become major league umpires. So it is in this chapter that I intend to give credit where credit is due.

Unlike the career of a professional baseball player, today's umpiring candidate must successfully complete the strenuous and demanding rigors of a reputable training school. Once he is properly trained and has paid his dues on the sandlots, a young umpire will begin his professional career in the low levels of the minor leagues. From that point, his hopes for advancement are no different from a player's. But it is at this initial level of pro baseball that he will be given a baptism by fire. Sure, it was a hardship for us minor league players to endure the long bus rides from town to town, but for these guys, who normally worked in two-man crews, traveling the back roads by automobile was even more tiresome. Even today, each ball club's schedule is set up with an equal number of home and road games, each road trip is followed by a homestand. However, the umpires never seem to catch a break. They are always on the road, living out of a suitcase, moving from one hotel to another, starting when they leave home in the spring and not ending until the season is completed. Regardless of where they are assigned to work, they never get to be the favorites of the home crowd and are always harassed and booed whenever a close call is made in favor of the visitors. But that's baseball, the way it was and the way it will be, until that dreaded day arrives when hi-tech replay cameras and robots take over the officiating duties. Yet to this day, it is the human element of umpiring that helps keep baseball as special and as near perfect as any game could be.

In the past century there have been almost 500 men who have worked as umpires in the major leagues and at the present time, only nine have been deemed worthy of membership in the National Baseball Hall of Fame. And while this handful represents the cream of the crop, I could quickly come up with a list of several others who deserve serious consideration for induction.

Among those immortals enshrined in Cooperstown and all of the other great arbiters in baseball history, none could have been more competent than the late Al Barlick. Al first became a National League umpire in 1940 when he was hired to fill in for "the father of all baseball umpires," Bill Klem, who was forced to take time off because of an illness. Al remained in the N.L. until retiring in 1971, securing a reputation for fairness, accuracy and integrity. Because of his loud animated calls, it was often said that every fan in the ballpark, even those in the most distant cheap seats would have no doubt about whether a player was safe or out whenever the decision was up to Al Barlick. However, after suffering a severe heart attack and missing two full seasons in 1956 and 1957, Al was back on the job at mid-season in 1958. Immediately after returning to his job, he worked what I remember as the finest game I ever saw an umpire call behind the plate. For a full nine innings in a game against the Braves in Milwaukee, there was not a single call of his that I could question. In every instance of that game, he seemed to make the proper decision. Fair or foul, ball or strike, safe or out, he was on top of every play. He was a great umpire who was at his best that day. After the final out of the game, I made a special effort to speak to Al as we were leaving the field. I commended him on his work and congratulated him for what I consider the finest job of umpiring I had ever seen. "Thanks, Hank," he responded in his typical humble manner. "Thanks a lot. It's just great to be back to work."

Al Barlick worked what I remember as the finest game I ever saw an umpire call behind the plate.

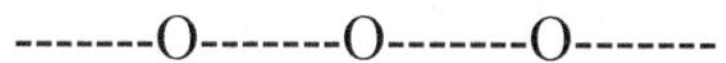

As a catcher, it was a big part of my job to familiarize myself with the umpires in my league and learn how to best use their individual preferences and tendencies in a way that would best serve my pitcher. Much of this involved consideration for the different strikezones found in the American and National Leagues. Traditionally speaking, the A.L. has always been known as a high strike league. Umpires there favor a strike zone, which runs from about mid-thigh up to the letters across the batter's shirt. On the other hand, N.L. umps prefer a lower strike, calling them only in the area starting just below the batter's knees and extending upward to his waist. In the National League, a strike is almost never called on a pitch above the belt, even though it may be located directly over the middle of the plate. While a big league player must be constantly aware of such details, most fans are never aware of many of the subtleties involved in a big league game. Naturally a batter's career can hang in the balance, based on his ability to hit a high or low pitch. However, the same principle can greatly affect the success of a pitcher.

Take for instance Sal Maglie, one of the great pitchers of the National League during the 1950s. He won consistently over the years, thanks in large part to his bread-and-butter pitch, a curveball that broke low in the strikezone, right below the batter's knees. But to his dismay, at mid-season in 1955, Sal was waived by the New York Giants and claimed by the Cleveland Indians. It was then that his career took a sudden and unexpected nose-dive. As soon as he landed in the American League, he found that his low sinking curve, the pitch that had served him so well for so long, was no longer effective. The strike zone there wasn't to his liking, as the A.L. umpires forced him to elevate his curve to heights where batters could pound his pitches like a blacksmith making a horseshoe! He failed to win a game while wearing an Indians' uniform. Yet the following year when he was sold to the Dodgers and returned to the National League, he went back to his old methods and found immediate success, winning 13 games and losing only five.

There was another distinctive contrast in American and National League umpires which involved their protective equipment. It was a big difference in their chest protectors used by home plate umpires that set them apart. Years ago it was only the umps in the N.L. who wore chest protectors inside their shirts when working behind the plate, while their A.L. counterparts were known for their outside balloon-type protectors. It wasn't until the late '70s that the A.L. abandoned that practice and had all new umpires entering the league use the inside model, as the veterans were permitted to take their pick. More often than not, umpires in the American League would place their hands under the balloon, raising it slightly to make it fit snuggly under the chin. Supposedly, this move would give added protection for the neck area, but prevented the ump from taking a low position over the catcher's shoulder. It is often claimed that this high posture is what led to the league's favor of high strikes. But who knows for sure? I was never convinced that the two styles of chest protectors were ever a factor in determining the limits of the strike zone.

Now there were cases in which the setup location used by certain home plate umpires definitely had a direct bearing on determining balls and strikes. As I went through the process of learning the quirks and habits of these fellows, I was willing to accept that each was different, with his own peculiar likes and dislikes. Their calls were always okay by me as long as they were consistent. Whenever I had problems with an umpire, it was usually due to his inconsistencies, which could put me and my pitcher in a no-win situation.

One ump who was always hanging over my shoulder, like a necktie on a windy day, was a true old-timer named Frank Dascoli. Frank was a longtime National League umpire, who like everyone else had his own idiosyncrasies. Yet he was dependable and I appreciated his consistency. As I squatted behind the plate and gave my pitcher a target, he would position himself over my shoulder, on the side which would be inside for the batter. His set-up location would provide him with a straight-on, close-up view of the inside corner of the plate, but at the same time it also compromised his view of the outside edge. Nevertheless, Frank was good to work with, as I always had a good idea about what to expect. With him behind me, I knew getting a strike called on the inside might be difficult. But he would usually ring up a strike if the pitch was away from a right-handed hitter and over the outer portion of the plate. Sometimes he would give us several extra inches of strike zone beyond the outside of the dish, so his calls all seemed to even out in the end.

Years ago there was a story about Frank going around that found its way to practically all clubhouses in the National League. The tale clearly illustrates the preference he had to work on the inside, even if it involved another line of work.

It was sometime during the late 1940s when Leo Durocher, Brooklyn's manager at the time, invited some of his well-known and influential friends to a social affair at the lavish Arizona home of (and likely at the expense of) one of his close well-to-do acquaintances. It was the kind of gathering that Leo loved to host. It was another chance for him to flaunt some of his Hollywood connections in front of his hand-picked baseball buddies. Among the partygoers were movie stars George Raft and Gary Cooper, along with Dodgers Bobby Bragan and Hugh Casey and for some curious reason, Leo's list included Frank Dascoli. Some of the ballplayers at the party brought back stories of how, during this evening of small talk and cocktails, Frank cornered Cooper and chewed his ear, begging and pleading for a role in his next Western movie. It was told that he had Gary trapped for about 20 minutes, pinned against the wall between his extended arms. Frank worked tirelessly to convince Gary that he was a natural actor with a special gift of handling horses. Some who were there described the situation as pathetic, while others said it was uncomfortable and embarrassing. However, Frank's efforts were all for naught. His hopes of being a cowboy film star blew away like a tumbleweed and his Wild West dreams went no further than Durocher's party, while the accounts of what happened spread all over baseball. That conversation was something Dascoli found difficult to leave behind in his dust. Making Cooper his captive audience would go on to haunt him for seasons to come and would resurface at the most inopportune times.

There would be games in which Frank worked where his calls were not palatable and shouts of displeasure would come from all over the ballpark which perpetuated the story. Years later in Pittsburgh, when cries of "Hi-ho, Silver!" came from the Pirates' dugout, Frank could take it no more. It was Bobby Bragan, our manager, who had been at Leo's Arizona party who was the loudest of all of the bench jockeys. As soon as Frank heard the Lone Ranger's famous rallying cry, he knew that it came from Bragan and knew what it implied. Frank wasted no time in ejecting Bobby from the game along with every player on the bench! As crazy as it sounds, only the guys in the bullpen were permitted to stay along with a coach and a batboy in the dugout. Everyone else wearing a Pirates' uniform was ordered to the clubhouse! Yet for the remainder of the night, Bragan continued to pull all of the strings, running the club through a telephone hookup with his bench coach, while watching the last few innings on a television set in his office.

It wasn't long thereafter that these same two unique personalities combined to create another crazy but unforgettable baseball moment. It was 1958 and Bobby Bragan was still at the helm of the Pirates and we were on the road in Milwaukee facing a tough Braves squad. It was a time when the weather was hot and our ball club was not. It was the end of July and we had a measly total of only 36 wins to show for our efforts. We were embroiled in yet another lost cause and Bobby had reached his limit. To this point the umpiring crew had put the Pirates on the short end of every call of the game. There had been a couple of questionable rulings from Frank Dascoli who was behind the plate, but the others in his crew -- Frank Secory, Stan Landes and Bill Baker -- were all doing a great job impersonating t*he Three Blind Mice*. I could tell Bobby wanted to give the quartet a piece of his mind, but he held back for just a few extra minutes. He kept his cool only long enough to order our clubhouse boy to dash off to the nearest concession stand and get back with a hotdog and a cold drink.

When the boy returned, Bobby grabbed his soda and frankfurter and stomped up the dugout steps and onto the field. At first he seemed to be heading in the direction of Secory at first base, when suddenly Frank popped up from behind home plate and ran to intercept him. Bragan stopped dead in his tracks when the two were only a few feet apart.

"Take it easy now, Bobby!" Dascoli ordered, attempting to defuse what he thought could become a volatile situation. "There's no call for you to be out here," he shouted.

For a moment Bobby stood like a statue, turning the confrontation into a staring contest. He glared at Frank as he slowly raised the cup to his mouth and drew a gulp of soda through the straw. "Here you go, Frank," he offered, "have some orange soda and while you're at it, take a bite of my hotdog too!"

Removing his mask from his face, Dascoli took a step back. "You're outta here, Bragan!" he barked. "Go take a shower, your day is over!" he declared, jerking the thumb of his right hand high in the air.

"That's just fine with me!" Bobby shouted back. "I think I'll go take a nap, Frank, just like you and your boys. You've all been dozing ever since this game started!"

Turning around and heading back towards the bench, Bobby knew continuing the argument would be futile. He took another bite from his hot dog and raised his cup to mock the jeering of the crowd.

This would be Bragan's final appearance in a Pittsburgh uniform as the curtain would come down on his stint as the Pirates' manager early the next morning. Perhaps he sensed his fate and knew that a dramatic exit was the way to go. Shortly after the game, our club filled two chartered buses and took off on a short 90-mile jaunt to Chicago to visit the Cubs. After arriving in the Windy City at 2:00 A.M., Bobby made a popular announcement to the team as we were stepping off the bus,"Go get'em, boys," he urged, "no curfew tonight!" I don't believe any of us saw Bobby the rest of the night, but within a few hours we learned of his firing. All it took was a phone call from our general manager, Joe Brown, and he was gone.

With our record, none of us could say the team's managerial move came as a big surprise. However, the change sure didn't pay off with immediate dividends. Under the leadership of our new interim skipper, Danny Murtaugh, we dropped all three games of that series at Wrigley Field to finish what had turned out to be a memorable yet dismal road trip. But for the Pirates, better days were ahead.

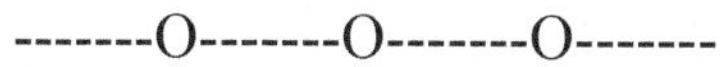

It wasn't very often that we had umpires traveling with any of the ballclubs, yet this particular trip was a little different. It was early April 1955 and I was a 25-year-old catcher who had just been promoted from Indianapolis of the American Association to the big league roster of the American League Champion Cleveland Indians. We had just broken training camp in Tucson, Arizona, and were enroute to Cleveland in preparation for the start of the regular season.

We were well underway on a flight that was smooth and uneventful. I had just pushed my seat back, closed my eyes and was all set to relax for the next couple of hours when I thought I heard someone calling my name. My eyes popped open as I wondered if my imagination was playing tricks on me. *Was I hearing things? Had I dozed off that quickly?* Before I could get resettled, I heard the same voice coming from behind me again. "Hank! Hey, Hank!"

I pushed down on the armrests raising myself from the seat. I turned and looked over my headrest and scanned the passengers to see just who it was that wanted my attention. Why, it was veteran umpire, Charlie Berry, seated in an aisle seat only a few rows back. He looked directly at me.

"Hey, you got a minute?" he asked. "Come on back here and let's talk," he offered.

"Sure, Charlie," I agreed. "I'd be happy to."

I made a few steps down the aisle toward the rear, to where Charlie was waiting and patting his hand on his armrest. "Have a seat right here, Hank. I know it's not very comfortable, but we won't keep you long," he assured.

At that moment I realized that the fellow next to him was Ed Runge, a member of Charlie's umpiring crew. Both of these fellows were veteran umpires in the American League on their way to work the season's opening game. "How's it going, Hank?" Ed asked as I continued to squirm, trying to balance my butt on the narrow arm of the seat.

"Just great, Ed," I smiled. All the while I'm wondering where this conversation was going. It's not very often that a couple of umpires call a young player aside for a chat. It was Charlie who broke the ice and got right to the point.

"Well, you know Hank, Ed and I were just talking about you and we decided that it might be good if we offered you a little advice. Now, you seem to be the kind of young fellow who makes the most of good advice and both of us would like to help you. We believe you have all the talent it takes to be a good catcher and we think your chances of having a long career in baseball are great, but there are a couple of things we should caution you about."

I began to squirm on the armrest as I detected the seriousness in Charlie's voice. "Sure, Charlie," I agreed. "I'm always open for a tip, tell me about it." Charlie seemed pleased with my reaction and slid a little further back into his seat before he continued.

"Okay, Hank, the first thing you need to remember is, we get paid to umpire, you don't."

I shook my head in agreement as I silently processed his advice. But still, I needed him to explain further.

"Now you seem to be doing a fine job behind the plate," he assured me. "And everyone is saying you do a good job handling your pitchers, but you need to leave the balls and strikes to us," he insisted. "You have a tendency to hold the ball in your mitt a bit too long whenever there's a call that you don't agree with and it's starting to wear a little thin with some of the umpires. We're just telling you this as a friend, Hank, because Ed and I think a lot of you and we don't want to see you get yourself into trouble if we can help you avoid it."

I continued to sit quietly, wanting to absorb as much from their advice as I could. "Yeah, fellows, I see what you mean," I finally responded. "I don't want to cause you guys any problems."

Both Charlie and Ed seemed relieved once they saw that their warnings were being received the way they had hoped. I could tell they were sincere, wanting to be helpful and to be constructive with their criticism.

I was just a 25-year-old catcher with the Indians when I received some great advice from two of the best umpires in the league.

"And there's another thing, Hank," Ed interjected. "Wait until you hear the third strike called before you go throwing the ball out to third base. None of us guys like to get shown up and there's nothing that shows up an umpire more than a catcher who fires the baseball to the third baseman when the pitch is called a ball! It's a simple thing, Hank, yet it's a way to save all of us a lot of frustration."

Charlie and Ed ended our talk by changing the subject. To be friendly, they asked a few of the normal-everyday questions such as, "Was I happy with the Cleveland ball club? and Did I expect to get in much playing time?" Finally, they both wished me well. I returned to my seat feeling a little surprised by their interest, yet grateful, knowing that these two fellows, two of the best umpires in the league, had taken their time to help direct me and keep me on the proper path. I was always thankful to them for their help and guidance and for the time they shared with me. It all helped to make me a better ballplayer.

To my friends, Charlie Berry and Ed Runge… Thanks, fellows. I miss you.

Both Charlie Berry and Ed Runge were featured on their own baseball cards in the mid-fifties.

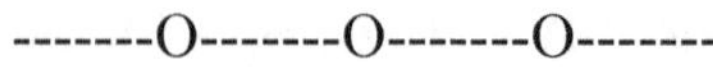

I haven't yet determined if being the first player in the major leagues to wear contact lenses was a blessing or a curse. Of course the style of contacts used back then was bothersome and not as comfortable as the lighter disposable ones used today, but still they were a big improvement over the heavy and sometimes dangerous eyeglasses that I had worn earlier in my career. The old contacts were costly and high maintenance and would sometimes pop out at the most inopportune times. This major drawback of the product is what leads me to this next story.

I first tried contacts when I was with the Pirates in the late 1950s, so when I landed in spring training with the Orioles in 1961, I had already adapted to wearing the thick rigid lenses. They had become just another part of my everyday game equipment, and had given me very few problems to this point. The novel idea of wearing them on the field had drawn a lot of attention from the press and brought lots of free publicity to my optometrist and my lens specialists. However, my streak of good fortune with contacts would extend only to our first exhibition game that spring, when we took on the Yankees in Miami.

For that first tilt of the Grapefruit League season, the Yankees used a tall imposing right-hander, who like me, was no stranger to the eye doctor. It was Ryne Duren, a veteran pitcher who was known as well for sailing his wild warm-up pitches against the backstop as he was for his signature eyeglasses, which were as thick as the bottoms of Coke bottles. Any hitter who stepped in against this bespectacled monster had to be on the lookout for a pitch over the heart of the plate as well as a fastball whizzing in the direction of the on-deck circle.

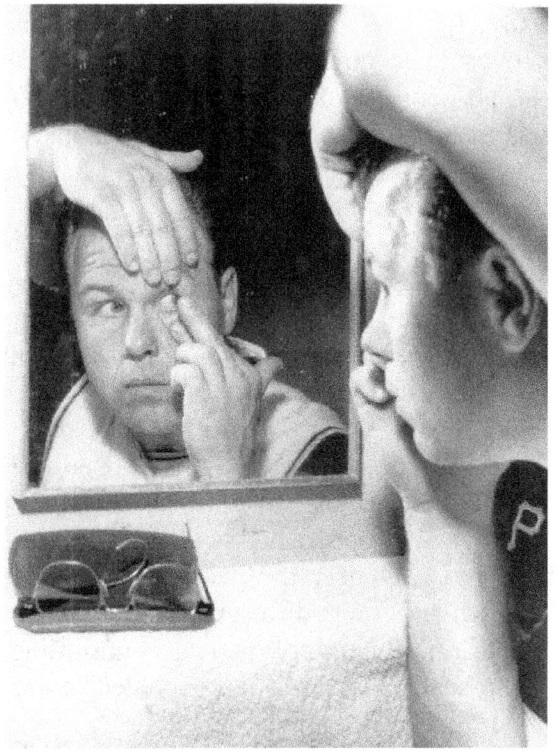

I first tried contact lenses when I was with Pittsburgh. They were just another part of my everyday game equipment.

I tossed the pine tar rag back inside the circle and walked toward the plate. As the first hitter of the inning, I continued to take a few practice cuts as I got closer to the batter's box. For once, the talkative Yankee catcher, Yogi Berra, was quiet as he took his place behind the dish, while Charlie Berry, the home plate umpire, readied himself for Duren's first delivery. I took one last brisk swing through the air and stepped up to the plate. I drew my bat back, holding it only inches off my right shoulder, poised and ready for the unexpected. Duren squinted and leaned forward, trying to get a read on Yogi's signal. That's when my troubles started, that's when the unexpected occurred.

Suddenly, the lens in my left eye popped out! Like a kernel of overheated popcorn, the tiny piece of round glass flipped out, glancing off of my cheek and down into the dirt! I hardly had time to blink before I realized what had happened.

"Time! Time!" I called, taking my right hand off the bat and raising my arm into the air.

"Time!" Charlie shouted just as the pitcher started into his motion. "What's the problem, Hank?" he asked, his eyes glaring at me through the bars of his mask. "Are you okay?"

"Yeah, Charlie," I assured him. "But, it's my contact lens, one of 'em just popped out and fell into the dirt here somewhere."

I stepped back out of the box and stooped over to get a closer look at the ground. Now with my hand covering my useless left eye, I dropped down on all fours and closely scanned the red clay near the plate. Yogi stood up, rising from his crouch and stepped closer to help with the search.

"We gotta find this thing! You can't go hitting with just one of those sealed beams," he concluded, comparing my contacts to headlights for an automobile.

The capacity crowd waited quietly, looking on as the hunt progressed. Charlie removed his mask and squatted outside the white lines of the box. He was as anxious as any of us to get back to the game. Duren, who had been waiting patiently, watching the escapade from the mound, had had enough. He started down the hill toward us. He appeared to be getting more agitated with each stride. "What's going on, Hank?" he snapped. "You lose a lens or something?"

"Yeah, Ryne, I sure did. It's gotta be here somewhere," I answered without looking up.

Duren came to a stop and stood a foot or two away from the front of home plate. He bent over slightly from the waist and peered down at the dirt through those odd looking ice-block glasses. "Here it is!" he announced, loud enough to be heard in the press box. He reached down and plucked up something from the ground. "Is this what you guys are lookin' for?" He reached over and handed me the elusive lens, the focus of this all-out search.

"It sure is, Ryne. Thanks for your help," I muttered, trying to hide my astonishment.

Not quite ready to go back to work, Charlie and Yogi were silent as they stared at each other in disbelief, both of them arriving at the same conclusion I had drawn. We had all realized that my tiny lens, which was not much bigger than a flake of snow, had been found effortlessly by the fellow known for having the worst vision in all of baseball!

Even with the recovered lens, I still wasn't ready to get back up to bat. My hands were dirty and sticky with pine tar, so I needed a little help from the team's trainer, Jimmy Ewell, and a few squirts of his saline solution to get the contact back in place. With that problem solved, I wished I could have said my troubles were over for the day. But on the contrary, my troubles were just starting.

In the late innings, my job behind the plate would become much more difficult. With Yankee runners on the base paths and our lead in jeopardy, our notorious knuckleballer, Hoyt Wilhelm, was summoned in from the bullpen. While this strategic move by our manager, Paul Richards, was definitely one that would strike fear into the hearts of opposing hitters, it was also one that meant nothing but trouble for me. In spite of resorting to the over-sized catcher's mitt, I still would have to put up a fight to keep that unusual pitch of his from floating past me and sailing back to the screen. With Wilhelm pitching, I often found myself lunging inside and then outside, trying to catch up with the ball, then having to drop to my knees to block one in the dirt. Over the course of just one or two innings, his unpredictable pitch would give me an exhausting workout!

With the first Yankee batter he faced, Hoyt tossed in one of his floaters which seemed to favor the inner half of the plate. I snapped the big mitt for what looked like an inside pitch only to find that the baseball took an unexpected break to the outside, striking the fingers on my unprotected right hand. To keep the Yankee runners from advancing, I fought to keep the ball in the dirt in front of me, but the damage had already been done. The impact had fractured the ring finger on my throwing hand, an injury which would eventually keep me out of action for more than four months!

Initially, the painful fracture was not set properly and soon it was apparent that it was not healing as it should. Thankfully, the Orioles were quick in making arrangements for me to visit Dr. Raymond M. Curtis, an internationally respected hand surgeon who practiced locally with his office in downtown Baltimore. His surgery and treatments were successful and proved to be vital to my recovery. There was no doubt that without his skill and expertise I would have been on the shelf a lot longer. It was just too bad that the surgery and lengthy recovery would only lead me to my next injury, another disappointing setback which was waiting right around the corner.

With fanfare that reached no farther than the doors on the Orioles' clubhouse, I was reinstated to the active roster while our team was on the road in Chicago. I drew the starting catcher assignment for the first game of a Saturday double header at Comisky Park. With two unproductive at-bats against Early Wynn, the ace of the White Sox pitching staff, I wasn't having the kind of game that would make headlines. Then, in the bottom of the sixth inning, through another unfortunate quirk of fate, a Chicago batter chopped down at an outside pitch, making only enough contact to force a foul tip down into the dirt, just to the side of home plate. The baseball struck the ground and spun upward, making another direct hit on my injury-prone right hand. The impact stung my index finger as if a thousand volts of electricity were passing through my arm. Thankfully, that batter made the final out of the inning and I could rush back to the dugout for relief. To help ease the pain, I used an old fashioned remedy and stuck my throbbing finger into a cold lemon, but I knew

I was hurt. With the sudden swelling and discoloration and my inability to bend the finger, I knew I needed to face reality and be prepared to sit out a few more games.

Luckily, the news wasn't so bad. My injury wasn't as serious as the previous one as tests showed there were no broken bones. But, while the swelling and soreness lingered for several days, I finally made it back into the lineup about a week later, in time for a weekend series in New York. The tenderness in my right hand was still giving me problems whenever I gripped a baseball to throw or squeezed the bat handle too firmly. Yet, over the weekend, I seemed to have found a comfortable grip as well as the perfect swing for the first game of the Sunday double header. That's when I managed to belt two long home runs to left field off a couple of the Yankees' most talented pitchers, Bill Stafford and Jim Coates.

After belting two long home runs in the first game of a Sunday doubleheader in New York, I'm celebrating with a couple of my Oriole teammates, Jim Gentile (left) and Steve Barber. We took two from the Yankees that day, 4-0 and 2-1.

At the plate, I was starting to hit my stride, but I needed to find a way to stay healthy for the rest of the season. If I could only keep my throwing hand out of the way of those nasty foul tips and find a safer way to handle the Wilhelm knuckler, I just might be okay. With a little luck, I could stay away from the foul balls, but trying to catch Wilhelm's floating butterfly pitch would be a tough job I couldn't escape.

Few sports fans today would have an idea of who I am referring to, if I mentioned the name Charlie Berry. But, that was not always the case. For more than four decades, Charlie was a favorite of football and baseball fans alike. He starred on the gridiron for Lafayette College and went directly to the NFL, at a time when professional football was in its infancy. He was a catcher for three American League baseball teams and served as a coach with the Philadelphia A's under hall of fame manager, Connie Mack. He saw no need to slow down after his career as an athlete was through and took a job as head football coach at Grove City College. He returned to the NFL as an on-field official for more than two decades and from there went back to baseball and became one of the most respected umpires in major league baseball. Needless to say, there aren't many sports figures in history who can match résumés with the late Charles Francis Berry of Phillipsburg, New Jersey. As an American League umpire, Charlie was nearing retirement when I joined the Orioles in 1961. Yet, with only a year to go before he would call it quits, he continued to work each game as diligently as if it were his first.

We had a pretty good ball club in Baltimore that year, finishing in third place, but well behind the front running Yankees. Our skipper, Paul Richards, a well-traveled ex-catcher himself, did a good job of finding ways to win ballgames. He had a knack for staying one move ahead of the opposing manager and getting the most out of his personnel. A key factor that helped us to a winning season was our fine pitching staff, which was composed of both experienced veterans such as Wilhelm and Hal Brown mixed in with a few talented young stars like Milt Pappas, Steve Barber and Chuck Estrada

Among the veteran hurlers on the club was Billy Hoeft, a tall southpaw who, like me, was in the twilight of a mediocre career. During his earlier seasons with the Detroit Tigers, Billy had been a consistent winner and could deliver a fastball as well as anyone in the league. However, at this point his fastball couldn't black your eye if he hit you with it, so he relied on a variety of pitches and often used his exceptional control to nibble at the corners of the plate.

It was that off-speed deliberate style of pitching that Billy used against Detroit in a September night game in Baltimore, when he began working himself into a jam. With umpire Charlie Berry behind the plate, Billy was struggling, having difficulty finding the strike zone. For the first several innings he had been sailing along with a three-run lead, but in the top of the sixth, Billy was beginning to pitch too fine, trying too hard to cut the black of the plate. After he missed the strike zone with seven balls in a row, I called for time and went out to the mound for a talk.

"Throw the ball over the plate, Billy!" I ordered. "Quit trying to paint the corners and let'em hit it. Let some of these guys out here work. We still have a good lead, so go for the middle of the plate. If they happen to hit it, that'll be okay, At least we'll have a chance to throw 'em out!"

A cloud of fine powder rose from the mound when Billy tossed the rosin bag aside. Without a word, he nodded in agreement just before I turned to go back to the plate. "Just throw me some strikes, Billy," I added as an after thought.

I got no farther than a few steps from the mound, when suddenly, another idea popped into my head. I spun right around and headed back to the hill to continue our discussion.

"Hey, there's something else you oughta' try," I offered. "Move over to the other end of the rubber and maybe that will help compensate for the miss."

I had no sooner finished my suggestion when I heard this booming voice come from behind me. It was Charlie.

"My gosh almighty!" he bellowed. "There're 35,000 people in the stands tonight and you two guys are out here dancin' around on the mound! Do you think we can get back to playing a ball game?"

"Sure, Charlie," I answered, as I started walking along beside him toward the plate.

"But, Charlie, all I wanted to do is get Hoeft to throw strikes," I explained. "I wanted to move him over on the rubber a little bit to try to help him out."

"Look at it this way, Hank," the crafty old arbiter responded. "If Hoeft can't throw strikes, Richards will bring in whoever is cranking up out there in the bullpen. So what's the problem?"

"Do you know who that is cranking up in the pen?" I countered. "It's Hoyt Wilhelm and I don't want to catch Wilhelm!"

Charlie stopped and stared at me, waiting to hear the rest of my story.

"You were there in Miami, Charlie, back in the spring when I was catching Wilhelm and he busted my finger and I don't want to catch him! I don't want to have to go through all of that again!"

"Okay, Hank," Charlie conceded. "I see what you mean. You got Hoeft out there on the mound who doesn't know where the ball is going to go…you got Wilhelm in the bull pen who doesn't know where the ball is going to go…the batter can't hit it…you can't catch it…and they want me to call it a ball or a strike! So, I'll tell you what…you go back out there and talk it over with Hoeft… and take all the time you need, because I don't know what else we can do!"

It's easy to see that Charlie was a great guy and a great umpire. The few extra moments he gave Billy and me was all we needed to make a few adjustments and work out of a tight situation. However, in baseball today, when it normally requires more than three hours to finish a nine-inning game, it would be helpful if some of the current umpires could take a few lessons from Charlie and use his style of officiating as an example for their own work. If the umpires of today controlled the pace and tempo of the game the way Charlie Berry did, the games would be shorter and the fans would be much happier. In a round-about sort of way, Charlie was a lot like me. He, too, loved baseball, but not when the game dragged on forever.

All in all, I would be quick to say that the umpires I knew were a great bunch of guys. But on the other side of the coin, there were times when I would encounter one who was a little too quick to let his ego get out of hand. Now keep in mind that an umpire is always there to be a neutral third party; he is never to show partiality and never to play favorites. Otherwise, he could play a big part in determining the outcome of the game. If an ump ever loses sight of this principle because he holds a grudge or feels that he needs to get even, I believe he is doing a great disservice to his profession.

One such individual who apparently lost focus on the high ideals associated with his job was National League umpire Bill Jackowski. Our relationship was never warm and friendly and it only seemed to get worse from there. The first run-in I had with Bill took place when both of us were in the class Triple-A, American Association. At that point in my career, I was quite confident that a jump up to the major leagues was just around the corner, but I believe Bill felt he had to do a little extra to reinforce his reputation to help increase his chances for a promotion.

One of the most important rules for all catchers is never purposely try to show up an umpire. On the field, the catcher should never expect the umpire to be his friend and should try to avoid doing anything to make him an enemy. So often in the heat of battle, differences between an umpire and catcher can be hashed out as long as the catcher doesn't turn his head during the discussion. Usually a catcher can plead his case and get in quite a bit of jawing, if he keeps looking out toward the pitcher. By the same token, the plate umpire can respond with his views in much the same manner. With both the catcher and ump restricting their body language and with both wearing protective masks, no one watching the game would ever know the pair is having a conversation, which is the main idea behind it all.

If you can visualize the strike zone as a rectangle, running the width of home plate and extending vertically from a batter's knees to his armpits, it may help explain the mounting frustration I experienced whenever Jackowski and I worked together. No matter where we were or who the Pirates were playing, Bill's strike zone would automatically shrink down to the size of a postage stamp as long as I was catching!

My dealings with Jackowski soured to the point where I approached our club's captain, shortstop Dick Groat, for some help. I urged Dick to speak to our manager Danny Murtaugh about the festering problem I had with Jackowski and to consider the idea of benching me whenever Bill worked the plate. "It'll be for the good of the club, Dick," I suggested. "I don't care what he does to me, I just don't want to see him hurt my pitcher!"

The pot finally boiled over in St. Louis during the early innings of a night game with the Cardinals. My pitcher, Bob Friend, a right-hander with great control, was consistently pounding the strike zone. Pitch after pitch, he would split the heart of the plate at a level between the hitter's knees and his belt and Jackowski refused to call any of them strikes. On a few of Bob's offerings, I held the ball momentarily in my glove at the very spot it was caught. Before taking the baseball from my mitt and throwing it back to the mound, I questioned Bill about his call. "Where was that one?" I insisted, as I continued to look in the direction of the pitcher. I got no reply. Bob's next pitch hit the same spot. Again I held the ball in my mitt and once more I asked, "Where was that one?"

Angrily Jackowski sprang from his position like a Jack-in-the-box. Before I could turn around to face him he had spun from behind the plate and was facing me. "You're outta the game, Foiles!" he screamed. "I've had about enough of you holding the ball and trying to show me up, so get outta here!"

Suddenly I realized this was the chance he had been anticipating for a long time. Seeing the unmistakable satisfaction he took in ejecting me was enough to push me over the edge. I squawked back at him, as my temper began to take the place of sound reasoning.

"You've had it in for me for a long time and you finally got a chance to do something about it!" I yelled. Then being careful not to make physical contact, I got even closer. I was right in his face. "Well it's not over, Jackowski! But, if you're man enough to finish this, you can meet me under the stands when this game is over!"

By this time Danny Murtaugh had dashed from the dugout, wanting to get to the scene before I got myself deeper into trouble. Coaches and umpires came running from all over, while the noisy crowd of Cardinal backers called me all sorts of names. They also shouted a few suggestions about an unpleasant place where they wanted me to go. But I was already hot, as I had never been more disgusted in my life!

Murtaugh took a stance directly in front of Jackowski, calling for an explanation. "Why did you run him?" he demanded to know. "Did he turn on you? Did he curse you?" Then, with their faces only inches apart, Danny barked again, "I want to know! Why did you run him?"

It was easy to see that Jackowski was struggling to come up with a solid response. Snatching his mask away from his face, he turned away from Danny and stared down at the ground. At this point he realized he has acted too hastily and didn't have a leg to stand on. "Tell me!" Danny continued to pry. "Did he turn on you or curse you? What did he do to deserve this?"

Bill knew he had painted himself into a corner, so he tried hard to swallow before he turned around to face Murtaugh. "Well, Danny, uh, no he didn't…he uh… you know, uh…"

With his hands on his hips, Danny held his ground, pressing the umpire for a straight answer. He glared sternly at Jackowski, as if he would give him all day to respond, if that was what he needed.

"Okay, Danny," Jackowski finally conceded. "I got tired of listening to him!"

My skipper shook his head in disbelief. He had had enough of this fellow. Disgusted by the absurd ruling and the lack of justification, Danny threw his hands down in frustration. "Well, I never heard anything like that before!" he countered as he headed back to the bench. "This guy beats 'em all," he mumbled.

I spent the remainder of the game in the clubhouse pacing the floor. Stripped to my undershirt and uniform pants, I walked back and forth in front of my locker. It was still burning me up, knowing I had done nothing to merit an ejection and would soon be slapped with a fine by the league office. *He's had it in for me since the minor leagues and I'm not letting him get away this. I can't wait until we meet after the game!*

Fortunately for both of us, Bill never bothered to show up under the stands. In the days that followed Warren Giles, president of the National League, had his office investigate the incident and after collecting the facts he needed, Giles ruled that there were no gross infractions and no justification for fining me. It was time for me to move on and do what was necessary to forget about Jackowski. Now, after all of these years, it's nothing more than water under the bridge.

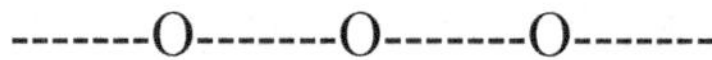

We can all recall instances in which the most qualified candidate didn't get the job, the best athlete didn't make the team or the best tasting pie didn't win the blue ribbon. And so it goes in baseball, whenever the most talented player doesn't make it to the big leagues and in some cases when the best umpire never gets a shot at the pros. That was precisely the case for my dear friend, Richard "Bullet" Alexander.

I first crossed paths with Bullet at a young age on the baseball diamonds, basketball courts and football fields of Tidewater. He was a native of the Cock Island section of Portsmouth, Virginia, and a graduate of Woodrow Wilson High School, where he was an all-around athlete for the Presidents, prime rivals of my beloved Blue Comets of Granby High. In spite of the many times we squared off as opponents on the athletic field, we became very close friends over the years, frequently working together, side by side in lodge activities as fellow Masons, fellow Shriners, as well as members of the Shriners Drum and Bugle Corps. After a long career of distinguished service to his native city, he retired as a captain from the Portsmouth Fire Department, making for a great loss, not only for me, personally, but for our entire community when we lost Bullet in December, 2009.

For almost a half century, he enjoyed a long career as an umpire, working at all levels of scholastic and collegiate baseball, community leagues and occasionally as high as Triple-A in the professional leagues. I have no doubt that had Bullet had the benefit of training at a credible school for umpires, he would have been a cinch to land a job with Major League Baseball. He was in his late seventies before he finally decided to hang up his whisk broom for good in 2007, ending many years of following his passion.

He reached the high point of his career when he was selected to umpire in the 1996 Summer Olympic Games in Atlanta. He often claimed that one of his biggest thrills was working the left field line in Atlanta-Fulton County Stadium for the final game of that tournament, as Cuba defeated Japan for the gold medal.

During the 1960s, when my time in pro baseball was behind me, I agreed to help out my cousin Roy Burton by doing a little managing and coaching for the team he sponsored in the Tidewater Summer League. Our team, the Burtons, won the league championship five years running, which made it a fun time for all of us. And during that stretch I enjoyed myself as much as any of the guys, inserting myself into a few games to play the outfield.

I recall one of our games in particular which was played there in Norfolk at the old Lakewood Field. It was a summer afternoon and to put it bluntly, it was as hot as the H*ammers of Hell!* To make conditions even more miserable, my friend Bullet, who was umpiring behind the plate, made what I took to be a terrible call and I wasn't about to let him get by with either his poor vision or his poor judgment! So, I called for time and rushed out onto the field, heading straight for Bullet. I yelled to him while we were still yards apart. "Are we watching the same game?" I growled. "You must be watching a different game, Bullet, because you really blew that one!"

"Don't get smart with me, Foiles!" he fired back. "I'll throw you outta here!"

"Go ahead and do it, Bullet," I challenged. "Go ahead and run me! Just run me!"

He turned and started to walk away, hoping I'd give up my argument and go back to the bench. He should've known better than that. He should've known there was more to come.

"You heard me, Bullet. I want you to run me!" I ranted. "Kick me outta here! 'Cause I've got a case of beer iced down in the boot of my car and I'll be happy to sit out there and drink a few cold ones while you boys finish this one up. Just let me know if that's what you want!"

"Now I see what you want, Hank," he quipped as he fought to turn back a smile. "I'm not going to run you out of this game," he declined in a much calmer voice. "I'm too smart for that. If I have to stay out here in this heat, you're gonna be out here with me!"

In the punishing heat, we both stayed there, on the field that summer afternoon, until the final out of the game was called.

Bullet was a terrific fellow, always working hard for good causes and always giving his time and energy for those in need. By the way, he was also great at being an umpire and even better at being a friend.

CHAPTER 13

OTHERS ALONG THE WAY

There aren't many stories in baseball that are more disheartening as the oft told story of my friend, Herb Score. And still today, while it is a story that keeps baseball fans asking "what if?" it is a story with a happy ending, one that will remind us that good things do happen to good people.

He burst onto the scene in 1955 as a much-heralded rookie pitcher with the Cleveland Indians. His pitching arm was like a flame-thrower as he consistently mowed down American League hitters with, what was, a record-setting strikeout rate for first-year pitchers. Reporters called him "a left-handed Bob Feller" and claimed that "the sky is the limit" for this blond devout Catholic boy from Rosedale, New York. And with his limitless potential, he was the overwhelming choice for the 1955 A.L. Rookie of the Year Award. However, his career as a player can be appropriately described as meteoric, in that his arrival in the major leagues filled the baseball world with a sparkling light, much brighter than what any young star had brought to the game in years. But, also like a meteor, his pitching brilliance was short-lived. After only two full seasons with the Indians, Herb's career as a player was dealt a horrific blow, one from which he would never fully recover.

It was in Cleveland Municipal Stadium on May 7, 1957, that Herb was struck in the face by a vicious line drive off the bat of Yankee infielder, Gil McDougald. It was a serious injury that crushed part of his nose and lacerated the eyelid and tissue surrounding his right eye. For weeks there was great concern that he could lose his vision in that eye or maybe even the eye itself. However, Herb Score was a battler, just as much off the field as on. His vision was spared and he recovered in time to take the mound for Cleveland in a handful of games before the end of the following season in 1958, meeting with a fair amount of success. Yet, many sportswriters and tellers of baseball stories would say that Herb was never again the same pitcher he had been prior to the injury, but that's where our opinions are different.

In the winter of 1958, I received a phone call from Herb who was living in the coastal town of Lake Worth, Florida. The months of recuperation and inactivity had made him eager to get back into action, but he first wanted to test himself, privately, to see if he still had what it took to pitch at the major league level. By this time, I had been with the Pirates for a couple of seasons, so we were no longer teammates, but that had had no bearing on our friendship. So that both of us could get a head start on spring training, he invited me to his place in Florida; he wanted me catch him and help him work his arm back into shape.

Together we found that Herb had not lost a single ounce off of his fastball. His arm was as strong as ever and his velocity was the same as it had been during his rookie year in Cleveland. With all signs looking up, we were both certain Herb would return to his old form and get back on track with his promising career. Unfortunately, we had no way of knowing that an off-season managerial change by the Indians would soon bring on his demise as a pitcher.

During his time as manager of the Pittsburgh Pirates, Bobby Bragan did a good job handling his personnel and proved himself as a great strategist, always thinking ahead and out guessing his opponents. On the other hand, the biggest complaint anyone had with Bobby was his tendency to misuse his pitchers. A reputation for being the type of manager who would "chew up a pitching staff" had already been hung on Bobby, well before he agreed to come to the Indians for the 1958 season. Serious arm injuries would sometimes result from his overworking his best hurlers and that's precisely what happened when he arrived in Cleveland and wanted to get the most out of Herb Score, the ace of his staff.

As early as our time together in the minor leagues, Herb would often complain about not being sufficiently warmed-up. After a lengthy workout, he would often claim that he still felt uncomfortable and uncoordinated. On occasions, he would laughingly confide that he wasn't ready to pitch and that he felt about as wild as a giraffe on roller-skates! Unfortunately, for guys like Herb, there were managers who didn't consider the fact that all pitchers are created differently, both physically and mentally. By disregarding the unique make up of an individual pitcher, a manager who is focused on winning can easily ruin a pitcher's career by not allowing him enough time to warm up, by pushing him in spite of an injury or by over use. Some managers are never aware of the harm they can do by moving a pitcher, who is normally a starter, to the bullpen, insisting that the pitcher instantly transform himself into an effective reliever. Sometimes it just won't work.

On a cold drizzly April day in Washington, Bragan directed Herb to go to the bullpen, wanting him to get loose before coming into the game as a relief pitcher, a totally new spot for Herb. Once he removed his jacket and started to throw, the rains came and cut short Herb's warm-up session. The game was then interrupted by the chilly intermittent showers and Herb was forced to retreat to the dugout in old Griffith Stadium to wait it out. There he sat with his teammates, waiting for the weather to improve while the cold dampness penetrated his body. Moments later when play resumed, he was up in the pen throwing again, and again his work was halted by another line of showers that passed through the nation's capital. Once more, when the rain clouds moved on he began to loosen up for the third time. The game resumed and he was stopped after just a few throws, when Bragan was seen on his way to the mound to make a pitching change.

Herb entered the game and pitched effectively, working three scoreless innings, striking out five of the first eight hitters he faced. Pitching like the Herb Score of old, he worked into the ninth inning where, after retiring the first two batters he delivered a pitch that sent a shocking pain through his left arm and down to his fingers. At the release point of his motion, he couldn't help but notice an audible "pop" in his elbow. He knew he was in trouble. Luckily, the pitch was popped up on the infield and caught for the final out of the game.

Herb left the pitcher's mound in pain and walked toward the dugout where he was met by Bragan.

"Nice work, Herb, good job!" he said, giving Herb a congratulatory handshake.

Herb accepted the compliments with his aching pitching arm hanging limp at his side.

"Thanks, Skipper," he answered. "But, I think I've hurt myself. It's my elbow … something popped on that last pitch and now I can't move it."

"Oh, don't worry about it, Herb, you'll be okay," Bobby assured him. "You'll be ready to go get 'em next time."

While still in Washington, a Senators' team physician examined Herb's arm. Days later he sought the opinion of an orthopedic specialist in Baltimore and received the same diagnosis. He had sustained severe damage to a tendon in his elbow, a debilitating injury for a pitcher, one that would require extended rest and possibly surgery. Yet, Herb was a fierce competitor who would try almost anything to avoid being out of the lineup. He tried his best to mask his injury and to keep pitching. He even altered his delivery in an attempt to lessen the stress and discomfort in his inflamed elbow.

From the first time I caught Herb in 1954 at Indianapolis, he had always come straight over the top with his pitching arm, a direct overhand delivery. However, with intense pain each time he tried to throw using his original form, he dropped his arm angle and began slinging the ball with a three-quarter or near side-arm motion. From being noted for having the best fastball in the game, Herb had been reduced to a mediocre pitcher, with erratic control and a fastball that was average, if that. After two fantastic seasons and a career filled with promise, it was sad to watch him fight to keep his job in the major leagues. It had been a short but incredible journey for Herb Score.

Apart from Herb's disappointing injuries, I continue to carry many fond memories of our times together as both teammates and roommates. Our enduring friendship, which started in Daytona Beach, Florida, in 1954, our first spring training together is one that stood the test of time. As a $60,000 bonus baby, Herb reported to camp with nothing more than a 100-mile-per-hour fastball, a good attitude and a big friendly smile. Born with as much natural talent as any pitcher ever had, he had no control and had no clue about how to throw a curve or a change-up.

In his first exhibition game that spring, I had the dubious job of trying to catch him, which was a real mission impossible! One of his pitches would whiz over my head and hit against the backstop, while the next one would skip away, striking the grass, halfway between the mound and home plate. He started the game by issuing a base on balls to each batter in the Richmond lineup…that's right, nine consecutive walks, without recording an out! It would have taken a *jack-in-the-box* to catch that guy! But thankfully, our prayers were answered, when in the second inning, the skies opened and blessed us with a pouring rain, heavy enough to wash out the remainder of the game.

After such a disastrous debut, Herb got some much-needed help from our pitching coach, Ted Wilkes, a former National League pitcher and veteran of many baseball wars. Ted had a knack for working with Herb. He started with the basics, teaching Herb the fundamentals of throwing breaking balls and off-speed pitches along with pointers that helped with his control. Before long, Herb was using these new pitches to complement his fastball, but still not with the confidence he needed. In tight situations he seemed tentative and tended to go back to his old ways, preferring to throw one fastball after another. It took some additional work with Ted, along with a little added pressure from me to give him the boost of confidence he needed to end the year as the American Association's Pitcher of the Year. Incidentally, he finished out the season with 330 strikeouts to go with a record of 22 wins and 5 losses.

Early in the year, I took the opportunity to help force Herb's self-confidence during a game with the Kansas City Blues. We held a comfortable lead over the Yankee farmhands; however, with a couple of runners on base, Herb started to look fidgety on the mound. With two men out, he worked the Kansas City hitter to a full count of three balls and two strikes before peering in to get my signal for the next pitch. With his glove resting on his right knee, Herb leaned forward, hiding the baseball behind his back. He was so certain that I would call for a fastball in that instance that he would have bet his paycheck. Even at 60 feet, six inches away from him, the surprised look on his face was unmistakable when he saw that I had dropped the signal for a curveball. Herb stared back at me from the mound, shaking his head for another sign. He straightened his body for a split second and shifted his weight forward. He leaned in again, hoping to see something different. Being careful to shield my signs from the base runners and opposing coaches, I put down the same sequence of fingers as before, still insisting on a curve. Now, beginning to get a little aggravated, the left-hander shook me off again. Squatting behind the plate, I kept my position, and for a third time I lowered my right hand between my legs, giving him the signal for his curve. This time I got no response. Herb just stood motionless on the hill staring at me as if I had lost my mind.

Noticing that we were unable to come to terms with our pitch selection, the fans started to grow antsy as a serenade of cat calls came from the box seats. Seconds later, Blues Stadium was filled with a roar of disapproval when I called for time and headed out to the mound.

Herb stepped down from the hill to meet me. "What are you doin', Hank?" he questioned. "It's 3 and 2!"

"I know what the count is, that's why I called for the curve!" I barked impatiently.

"I've never done that before," he admitted. "I've never thrown it on 3 and 2."

"Well, now's as good a time as any!" I shot back.

Getting in the last word, I turned my back and trotted toward the plate. Without giving Herb time to think about it, I quickly squatted down and gave the sign for a curve. The batter hardly had time to settle into his stance before Herb accepted my call. This time he nodded in agreement.

Working from the stretch, Herb came home with the pitch. Considerably slower than his trademark pitch, his curve sailed in toward the plate about shoulder-high. The unsuspecting hitter started to take his stride. He wanted to go for the high one, but suddenly he held back. Instantly, the baseball dropped low and broke inside. It was too late for him to swing. All he could do was bend slightly at his knees and groan, as the spinning ball sank into my mitt. "Strike three!" the umpire yelled. "You're out!" The inning was over and we were out of the jam.

That one curveball did more to bolster Herb's confidence than anyone can imagine. After that particular game, he quit throwing the ball and became a more polished pitcher. In the months that followed, he came to rely more and more on his curveball, as well as his newly-learned change-up. He took his effective variety of pitches with him to the major leagues where they were soon legendary. But, it was his fastball that made his name and it is his fastball that continues to be a summer topic in barbershops and a winter time subject for hot stove leagues.

Herb Score receives my congratulations after hurling a 16-strikeout masterpiece against Boston on May 1, 1955. His performance included 9 strikeouts in the first three innings!

"The next Bob Feller?" some older fans wonder. "A Sandy Koufax before there was a Koufax," others speculate. But maybe we should be content to simply call him "the one and only Herb Score." A gracious man he was, never one to look back on his career with regret or misgivings. Herb was one who always focused on the positive.

On the radio with the Cleveland Indians broadcast team for decades, Herb added insight, color and sometimes comedy to every game. His commentary gave listeners a vivid mental picture, as well as opinions based on the knowledge and experience he gained from his time in the sport. Yet, he seldom spoke of his own career and never referred to any of his own personal accomplishments. One of the few times he ever spoke on the air concerning his talent was when he wistfully commented during a close game, "I'm just glad I was not up to bat in this situation…'cause I never was much of a hitter!"

Yes, sir. That sure sounds like the Herb Score I used to know.

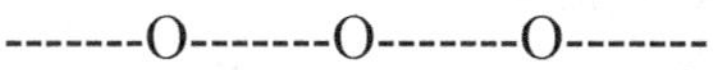

For a couple of seasons in the late 50s, I had the pleasure of being teammates with one of the more colorful personalities ever in baseball. His unique personality, his ego, his physical size and his tape-measure home runs all made Dick Stuart a player I'll never forget. I first met Dick when he came up to the Pirates as a rookie in 1958 and if there ever there was an award for the brashest newcomer to reach the big leagues, I would have to list Dick among the finalists.

It had only been two years earlier that he set some sort of record for home runs, slugging 66 round-trippers while playing for Lincoln in the class A Western League. Regardless of the classification, hitting that many homers at any level in pro baseball is an incredible accomplishment, worthy of bold print in any baseball record book. Yet, Dick took it upon himself to make sure that no one got a chance to overlook his feat.

Prior to his promotion to Pittsburgh, we had all heard about Dick and the impressive home run numbers he had produced at each level of the Pirates' farm system. Still, none of us veterans were quite ready for a rookie who obliged autograph seekers by dotting the "i" in Dick with a star and adding a "#66" below his signature as a means of calling attention to his home run mark. Then, too, the guys in the Pirates' clubhouse weren't prepared for a young player who, at 6'-4" and 220 pounds, concentrated only on hitting the ball out of the ballpark and had no regard for the defensive aspect of his game. Year after year, Dick was always among the first sackers who committed the most errors, an annual trend that never seemed to bother him. And although it was great having his explosive bat in the middle of our batting order, his lack of defensive prowess would sometimes cost us the game. In many cases his errors were painful to watch. Some of his plays at first base could have been handled more efficiently by the neighborhood butcher. But rather than take it to heart, making jokes out of his frustrating miscues would sometimes help ease the tension on the bench. Once, when retuning to the dugout after a disastrous inning in the field, Dick was met by a Pittsburgh teammate reclining on the bench, laughing and wearing a glove on each hand and one on each of his feet!

Throughout his career, Dick had executives, general managers and managers running numbers to compare the value of his high RBI totals against the cost of the excessive number of runs that scored on his misplays in the field. Most fans had never seen a player who could do so much with his bat and had no idea what to do with his glove. Because of his ineptness at first base, fans tagged him with the nickname, "Dr. Strangeglove," a comical take-off from a popular 1964 Peter Sellers movie. Those fans who were delighted to see Dick clear the bases with an extra-base hit or a long homer were the same fans that cringed whenever an infield pop-up or grounder came his way. Once, on a windy day in Boston's Fenway Park, he received a standing ovation from the crowd when a hot dog wrapper blew across the grass, to the right side of the infield. Dick walked over, snatched the crumpled paper from the turf and stuffed it in his hip pocket. For many, it was the first time they had ever seen him catch anything!

We were together for two seasons in Pittsburgh, and I'll have to admit that Dick was one of the more unique teammates I can recall. He was quite friendly, yet he seemed to move to the beat of a different drummer. He was always in a hurry and going his own way. He was the last to arrive at the clubhouse and the first to leave. There was never anyone in pro baseball that could shower and get away from the ballpark faster than Dick. Some of the players with lockers nearby would question him about his quick showers, asking him if he did, in fact, use soap! He was a spiffy dresser, up on the current fashions, and the brands he wore were top-of-the-line. Game after game, we noticed how he rushed through his routine to get himself ready for a night on the town. Everything had to be perfect, from his hair down to his feet.

Of all the fellows on the club, no one watched Dick more closely than Don Hoak, our slick fielding third baseman. While getting himself dressed, Don couldn't help but peer over at Dick and observe his daily rituals of dressing and grooming. It was Don who was watching closely enough to notice how Dick's shoes were always perfectly placed on the floor beside the stool, so that without getting up, and with the aid of a long handled shoehorn, Dick could slip into them with no wasted motion. On this particular day, it was Don again, who noticed the shiny new pair of expensive black-n-whites that Dick pulled from the shoebox and placed in the usual place in front of his locker. Unexpectedly Dick got up and left, just walked away, perhaps to make a call or maybe to use the restroom.

Like a gambler with an ace up his sleeve, Don immediately got up from his locker and started making the rounds. "Hey, boys, we need to teach this fellow a lesson. Gimme ten bucks and hurry up. Gimme ten," he prodded each of us. Now, we had all known ol' fun-loving Don Hoak long enough to know that the deal he was about to pull off would be a good one, a prank well worth the price of admission. So, we each handed Don our hard-earned money, no questions asked. By canvassing only a small portion of the room, he collected sixty dollars in almost no time. He wound the money into a tight roll and pushed the paper bills deep into his pocket.

Trying to use what's left of my memory, I recall that the locker room floor in old Forbes Field was nothing more than a grid of sunken wooden blocks or pilings. They looked similar to tiles, with dirt filling used between the squares. Also, there were tall swivel-type stools which were fastened securely to the floor in front of each locker. The unusual type of flooring was just perfect for what Hoak had in mind.

During the few short minutes that Dick was away, Don had all the time he needed to execute his caper. He went about his work like Santa Claus, about to fill stockings with sleeping children in the next room. We continued to watch as he eyed the new shoes in front of Dick's locker. After a few seconds of contemplation, he stepped back over to his own locker, reached in and pulled out a hammer and a couple of nails.

Showing the skill of an experienced carpenter, Don drove a twenty-penny nail through the bottom of each of Dick's new shoes! Through the leather soles and deep into the thick wood flooring, the nails were driven down until their heads were flat on the inside of each shoe. With his job complete, Don scurried back to his stool, where he sat with his arms folded across his chest, as contented as the cat that had just swallowed a canary.

Within seconds, Dick returned and on cue, he hopped up on his stool to finish getting dressed. Unaware of his audience, he hurriedly went about his business, buttoning his shirt and stuffing his shirt tail into his trousers. He glanced at his wristwatch, adjusted his pressed collar and admiringly rubbed his fingers along the sharp crease in his pants. Spinning his seat around to face the locker, he aligned himself for easy access to his shoes and without rising from the chair, he reached down with his long shoehorn and guided his feet into the lavish new two-tones. Then came the moment we had all paid to see.

Realizing he would be late for his date, Dick sprung up and out of his chair. He reached an upright position and suddenly discovered he could not move his feet! He tried again and again, one foot and then the other. A look of confusion came to his face. Suddenly, it hit him; he knew he was a victim of the notorious clubhouse prankster! Dick's face grew red; his blood was boiling as he looked around and learned that he had been the source of so much amusement. Pitcher, Ronnie Kline, fellow catcher, Danny Kravitz and the rest of the boys were all cracking up

"What have you done?" he screamed, veins bulging in his neck. "You miserable bunch of SOBs…you've ruined my new shoes!"

Aware that we had a hulking 25-year-old who was about to go bananas, Don stepped forward and owned up to his mischief.

"Okay, Stu, just take it easy," Don consoled him. "We're just having fun and trying to teach you a little lesson at the same time."

"Some lesson!" Dick shouted back angrily. "What about my new shoes, they're ruined! And how am I going to pry them off the floor?"

Don stepped closer and pulled a screwdriver from his hip pocket. "No problem, Dick," he assured. "We'll have'em loose in just a second."

Moments later, Hoak was holding the damaged footwear in one hand as he dug into his trousers for the money. He shoved the roll of bills into Dick's shirt pocket.

"Well, give'em back to me," Dick pleaded, reaching for the shoes. "I've gotta get out of here."

"Not so fast," Don cautioned. "There're sixty bucks in your pocket, so the shoes belong to us now."

Almost in tears, Dick wasn't quite sure how to handle the situation. Still relatively new to the big leagues and still full of himself, he had just been brought back down to earth by veterans who had seen many cocky young players come and go over the years. But, this case was a little different from any we had witnessed before. This was the first and only time any of us could recall watching a cocky, well-dressed young man like Dick leave the clubhouse for a hot date with a pair of ugly wooden shower clogs on his feet!

With a lot of years in professional baseball and well over 200 major league home runs, Dick Stuart was certainly a tremendous hitter, a real fencebuster during his time. It's unfortunate that his playing days were over before the advent of the designated hitter. Otherwise, he may have been one of the best. Dick was also a good fellow and always a lot of fun.

With well over 200 career home runs Dick Stuart was a tremendous hitter and was always a lot of fun.

CHAPTER 14

MY FAVORITE "STOREYS"

Even a team's most successful road trip could be very tiresome and lonely. With the long hours spent traveling, the restaurant food and living out of a suitcase for days on end, the grind of life on the road is enough to give anyone a hankering for a good night's sleep in his own bed and a hot home-cooked meal. Personally, with my wife Joyce and two sons, Hank and Marc, at home, things could sometimes get stressful for all of us when I was away. But Joyce and I soon realized that our hectic home life, with two young boys couldn't be put on hold every time I left to go on the road. And I must add that she did a remarkable job of holding down the fort and managing so many family situations on her own over the course of my career.

After nearly two weeks on the road, everyone on the ball club was anxious to get back home to Pittsburgh. We were pleased to be playing .500 baseball on this western road swing, but all of us had gotten our fill of trains and hotels. After catching a few short cat naps on the train, we pulled into Cincinnati around 2 A.M. for what would be our last stop before heading home. It was sometime after three o'clock before we finally got in our hotel rooms, yet I managed to get a few more hours of sleep before getting up to go grab a late breakfast. I wasn't pressed for time, so I took it easy. It was early afternoon when I returned to my room where I relaxed there for a while, wrote a couple of letters and made a few phone calls before deciding to go out for a beer at the Rendezvous, one of our team's regular watering holes, not far from the hotel.

I was enjoying a cold mug of brew and was catching up on some of the latest news with my friend, Dino, the bartender when a well-dressed, middle-aged couple walked in and seated themselves at the bar, around the corner from me. We exchanged pleasantries and introduced ourselves. I learned that I was in the company of Jack and Nina Storey.

Our conversation began with the usual small talk when I noticed that he was distracted. Jack was eyeing my Masonic ring.

"I see that you are a traveling man," he remarked.

"Yes, indeed, Jack, you're quite right. I'm with Lodge number 164 out of Norfolk, Virginia."

Jack nodded with approval before continuing. "So what brings you to Cincinnati, my brother, business or pleasure?"

I explained that I was in town for work and because I was with the Pittsburgh Pirates, I would be in town only for a couple of days. My response got little reaction from Jack, as he took another glance at my ring. He was attentive, but I could tell that he had more questions. He proceeded to ask about my family back home in Virginia and wanted to know the last time I had sat down to a home-cooked meal.

"And what are your plans for this evening?" he continued.

"Nothing special tonight, Jack," I confessed. "In just a few minutes, I think I'll head back over to the hotel to shave and shower and then I'll go out to dinner with some of the fellows on the team. After that, we might hang around downtown to catch a movie. I'm not really sure, but since we don't have a game, I'm just hoping to have a quiet evening."

Jack got up from his barstool, politely excused himself and walked toward the restroom. "Don't go anywhere, Hank," he urged, looking over his shoulder. "I'll be back in just a couple of minutes."

Moments later, I spotted Jack across the room; he was using the public telephone. After a short conversation he returned to the bar and stood next to my stool.

"Well, Hank, we are going to leave now, but before we go, we have a request. Nina and I would be honored to have you join us later this evening for dinner at our home. We realize this idea is very impromptu, but we would welcome your company. And, as I mentioned to you earlier, I'm an artist and I would be pleased to show you some of my paintings."

Jack knew that I was caught unawares by their invitation and with his hat in one hand, he placed the other on my shoulder while he waited for an answer. They seemed like such a wonderful couple, yet I was hesitant to accept. I surely didn't want to cause them any inconvenience.

"Come on, Hank," he tried again, "we would really enjoy your visit."

"I can't do that, Jack," I responded. "I can't impose on you folks like that."

"You can't impose on a brother," he said emphatically. "Besides, I just called our house and made arrangements with our maid. She will have everything prepared for us, if you will agree to come. It would be a disservice to us if you didn't accept."

Without thinking, I took a quick sip from my mug and placed it back on the bar. "Okay, Jack, that will be great," I agreed. "If you're sure I won't be putting you to too much trouble."

"No trouble at all," he assured me. "Just take your time and finish your beer. Then go back to your hotel, as you planned and get dressed. And keep in mind, Hank, this will be very informal, so just put on a sport shirt, there'll be no need for a coat and tie. When you're ready, come back here to the Rendezvous and give us a call. We'll drive over and pick you up." He quickly scribbled his phone number on a bar napkin and handed it to me as he reached to shake my hand. "We'll be waiting to hear from you," he said, affirming our plans. "We'll look forward to a great evening together."

With Jack behind the wheel, the drive from the bar over to his home took only a few minutes. He knew the area well and pointed out the elegant Victorian architecture of some of the old houses that lined the streets of his neighborhood. Finally, he turned off Upland Place and pulled into the driveway of a large, stately, grey-stone house.

"Well, here we are," he announced. "We have a little while before dinner, so let's go inside and I'll fix us a drink, and then I'll show you around."

Their home was gorgeous! All told, there were 22 rooms, including art studios for both his students and himself. What he hadn't mention earlier, was that he was among the top five commercial artists in the country and with that, he was the administrator of his own private college, The Central Academy of Commercial Art. With both my gracious host and hostess, I toured their spacious studios and galleries, viewing some of the most spectacular artwork I had ever seen. Jack specialized in American Western and still life, painting people, animals and inanimate objects with incredible color, clarity and detail. In particular, I recall a large painting of his, which was that of a downtrodden drunk. The picture was so unbelievably lifelike that I thought I had gotten a whiff of the booze and garlic from the poor fellow's breath!

We enjoyed a most delicious meal together in the dining room, followed by more intriguing conversation and a few more adult beverages. The hours went by much too quickly. It had been a truly special evening and because of their generous hospitality, I felt that I should repay them in some small way.

"Do the two of you ever go out to Crosley Field and see a ballgame when the Reds are home?" I asked. "If you haven't, I'm sure it would be something that both of you would enjoy."

Jack and Nina confessed that while they had lived in the Queen City for many years, taking in a Reds game is something they had planned to do. "It's just one of those things we never got around to doing," Jack admitted.

"Well, I hope that you both are free tomorrow night," I hinted. "I would like to invite both of you to come out to the ballpark, as my guests. I will see that there are tickets waiting for you, and after the game, I would like to take you out for dinner, anywhere you would like to go, just name the place." Without either of them being fans of baseball, they enjoyed the game and after a pleasant dinner out on the town, we agreed to stay in touch.

Over the years, Jack and Nina Storey proved to be true friends, not just to me, but also for Joyce and the boys. Whenever I was traveling on the road and the team stopped in Cincinnati, we made it a point to visit and share time together.

It is a proven fact that you can never tell where a career in professional baseball will lead you. After leaving the Pirates, I was dealt back into the American League where I had a brief stay with Kansas City. Then it was back to Pittsburgh and on to Cleveland, Detroit and Baltimore. After all of that moving, I should've considered taking a job with the auto club! Yet throughout my career, each time I was traded, released or my contract was sold to another club, I always found that there were both positive and negative points associated with the change. And when I was purchased by the Reds in the spring of 1962, my family and I were faced, once again, with the headaches of packing up and moving to another town. But this time it was a little easier for all of us to find a bright spot in the fray, as we knew this move would put us closer to our friends, Jack and Nina in Cincinnati.

During the year and a half I was with the Reds, we got to visit with the Storeys quite often. Occasionally we would dine out, but our boys preferred our outdoor barbeques.

Incidentally, whenever I was on the road, Jack and Nina never once failed to call Joyce, just to check on her to see if there was anything they could do to help out.

Today, there is a beautiful framed painting, hanging in our home; it is what Jack often called his "rendition of the perfect quarter horse." Although we still appreciate his masterful handiwork, to Joyce and me, the picture is much more than fine art. It is a symbol of a special friendship that came to us through baseball. And though Jack and Nina Storey were wonderful friends, they weren't baseball people at all. They were just some of the other great people along the way.

CHAPTER 15

BRUSHES WITH HOLLYWOOD

As I pointed out in earlier chapters, many major changes have been imposed on professional baseball which have not only affected the way the game is played, but also changed the lifestyle of the players. With the outrageous salaries and benefits earned by players today, current big leaguers can leave the game financially set for life. Retired players are no longer pressed to start another career after leaving baseball, nor is it necessary for them to hold down an off-season job each year during the fall and winter months.

However, after reflecting back on my own career, I'll have to admit I didn't have it bad at all. I was fortunate enough to have landed some off-season work that I truly enjoyed. In particular, there was one such job which took me cross-country, to the entertainment capital of the world. With that job, I found exciting experiences, made some new friends and returned home with the kind of memories that last a lifetime.

Over the course of five consecutive winters, I had the pleasure of working under the direction of Tom Chisman, founder, owner and president of WVEC-TV, our local ABC Television affiliate in Virginia's Tidewater area. Primarily, I worked out of the station's headquarters office in Hampton as a Promotions Manager, yet I found myself doing almost anything that needed to done within the company. I made public appearances to promote some of the station's products and programs. I sometimes wrote scripts for some of our local programming. Why, I even appeared in my own on-air commercial for a locally manufactured waterproofing compound called *Bil-Dry, Grip-On.* And though I used my best promotional talents to hawk the product during halftime of the Sun Bowl football game, I never figured out just how successful my sales pitch actually was: "Oh, and did I forget to mention? It's available in four popular colors. Just be sure to ask for it by name at your favorite paint or hardware store. That's...*Bil-Dry, Grip-On*! Get some today!"

By 1962, the once popular TV Western, *Wagon Train,* which had run its course on the NBC network, was seeing its ratings plummet. During the show's first season on ABC, its slipping popularity had network executives scrambling for new ideas. The folks at ABC decided to keep the program for another couple of seasons and allow it to flounder and die a slow death on its own. All the while, they had a plan for a fresh new show with a cast that included some bright young stars who were in the beginning stages of notable show business careers. In keeping with the frontier theme of covered wagons heading west, ABC producers began shooting episodes of their new series titled *The Travels of Jaimie McPheeters.*

.

With a young Kurt Russell in the lead role as Jaimie and rugged upstart actor, Charles Bronson under contract, the project was off and running. ABC was also excited to have an early version of the Osmond Brothers signed up as part of the cast. The Osmonds took on roles as members of the singing Kissel family, pioneer brothers who would sometimes perform their musical numbers. With an incredibly talented cast and a sure-fire theme, the network was certain they had a hit series on their hands.

Back home on the local scene, ABC was calling for our station, and all other network affiliates, to go on an all-out campaign promoting the new show. Promotional staffs at each station were ordered to make *The Travels of Jaimie McPheeters* a priority and to do whatever was needed to make it a success. It wasn't long before our boss, Tom Chisman and a few of us at WVEC-TV came up with a plan to make it happen. "What would be better than having someone on location?" Tom proposed.

We checked the schedule for the upcoming baseball season and discovered that once the Reds broke training camp in Tampa, we had just one game in Cincinnati before heading out on a West Coast swing to Los Angeles and San Francisco. Our stop in L.A. would put me only minutes away from MGM's Television Studios in Culver City, creating a great opportunity for me to visit the set of the new show. I couldn't wait for the baseball season to start.

Production and taping of the initial episodes were well underway when I arrived. My job, if you could call it that, was to observe the film crews as they went about their work and to grasp the theme and storylines for the series. Essentially, I was there to gather in anything that might be helpful with the promotional work going on back at the station.

In particular, I was captured by the talents of Kurt Russell, a 12-year-old towhead, who was the perfect choice for the part. Kurt was a delightful kid, full of energy and always on the move. He seemed very confident in his work, always knew his lines well and was receptive to directions on the set. Yet, for a child actor in a starring role, I detected no arrogance or conceit like you might expect from a youngster in his place. During breaks he talked with everyone, including me. That's how I learned he was a big baseball fan.

Naturally, Kurt was a Dodger fan, but, like any courteous young man would have done, he admitted to liking the Cincinnati Reds a little bit too. He explained how he enjoyed his acting work, but that his big goal in life was to be a major league baseball player. "I'd sure like to play for the

Dodgers," he confided. "Being a pitcher would be great, or maybe a shortstop, or maybe a second baseman."

Young Kurt and I talked at length about his hopes of turning pro, while a photographer from ABC snapped a few shots of us chatting. He suggested that we pose for a publicity still, with one of the studio's covered wagons as a backdrop. After that Kurt and I were pals for sure. He was thrilled by my offer of box seats behind the Reds dugout the next time we were back in town. A gift of a million bucks would not have excited him more.

A few weeks passed and the Reds and I were back in Los Angeles for a three-game set. I remembered my invitation to Kurt and was certain to keep my word. He received the tickets I had promised and was there in his box seat well before game time. We were both happy that he was there in time to see me smash a 3-run homer off Dodger left-hander, Johnny Podres in the first inning. And while this all took place in enemy territory, it was great to know that I had at least one fan there in Dodger Stadium cheering me on, a handsome, moppy-head kid behind our dugout, who was yelling his heart out!

In the years that soon followed, Kurt learned just how close he would come to seeing his "other dream" become a reality. In the early 1970s, when his career as an actor was taking off for the stars, he took time away from his work to pursue his enduring passion to play baseball. And though he never became a Dodger, he was heavily scouted and was signed by the California Angels to play in their minor league system. Primarily a second baseman for three professional seasons, he showed himself to be a talented hitter, yet he never measured up to major league standards. But, that's not to say that Kurt Russell was never heard from again.

While ABC's pet project, *The Travels of Jaimie McPheeters* lasted only one season, Kurt went on to create a personal filmography of hit movies as long as a Hollywood limousine and he continues to work today as one of the most revered actors in film history. From *The Computer Wore Tennis Shoes* to *Tombstone* and from *Overboard* to *Backdraft*, I have always been entertained by his films and continue to be a fan of his. But, I wonder, could he still be a fan of mine?

There was that wonderful time, years ago when he told me about his hopes and dreams and I am flattered to think that my advice encouraged him to give baseball a try, when the opportunity finally came. But back in 1962, we exchanged autographed photos, and now, somewhere among my stacks of old curled up pictures, there are a couple of signed black and whites, which show the of the two of us posed beside a covered wagon. On one, in faded ballpoint, he noted, "Thanks for taking these pictures with me – Kurt." The other is a simple illustration of how important baseball can be to a young boy. On that photo he inscribed, "You sure hit a long home run – Kurt"

Today, it's great just to look back and see how both of us have lived out our dreams.

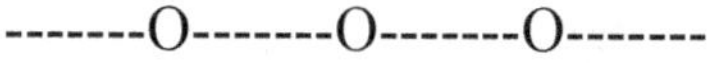

There could never be a more beautiful place to live than Waikiki Beach in Honolulu, Hawaii. Each day, when I peered out my window of the brand new Ilikai Hotel and looked out over the sand and sea, I could never really say for sure which provided a richer shade of blue, the water or the sky. But still, I was living alone and eager for my family to arrive. It was almost time for school to be out for the summer, so I knew Joyce and the boys would soon be flying out to join me in this paradise in the Pacific.

Naturally, Kurt was a Dodger fan, but, like any courteous young man would have done, he admitted to liking the Cincinnati Reds a little bit, too.

But, this was 1964 and I couldn't help from seeing the handwriting on the wall. I was about to turn 35 years old and that's much too old for a catcher to be fighting for a job. I was still property of the Los Angeles Angels, and after seeing limited action with the Halos the year before, I was relegated to the Hawaii Islanders, their triple-A club in the Pacific Coast league. Seeing that the entire Angel organization was fully loaded with promising prospects at all levels, I knew my days as an active player were numbered. Except for a few other veterans on the team, like infielder Herb Plews and pitcher, Mickey McDermott, the Islanders' roster comprised mostly young fellows, still in their twenties, jockeying for positions on the big league club.

The smells of fresh paint and new carpet filled the air as I passed the front desk on my way to the main entrance to catch a cab to the stadium. The elegant and spacious lobby was buzzing with staff and guests, as it had every day since I first registered. The place had been billed as the first high-rise luxury hotel in Hawaii, and with a full occupancy of guests from every walk of life, the Ilikai was the new center of activity in downtown Honolulu. When it came to those you might find registered there, the possibilities were limitless. Suddenly, I heard someone call my name. "Hey, Hank!" a voice called from behind me. "Hank, wait up!" I stopped and turned to see who it could be. As a professional baseball player, it's hard to guess who it is that will ask for a moment of your time.

It was Ralph Volpe, a friend I had met in the Los Angeles area a couple of years back, where he had been involved in the movie business as some sort of a technical hand. He was hurrying toward me with a big smile, swinging his briefcase with each step. "It sure is a surprise to see you, Hank," he continued. "How are you and what brings you out here to the islands?"

I was equally surprised by our meeting and paused for a moment to recall his name. "Oh, hi, Ralph, it's good to see ya', my friend," I responded tentatively. His hearty handshake was a relief, assuring me that I had been correct with his name. "I'm doin' great. I'm in town playing ball for the Islanders and on my way to the stadium now. What about you?" I asked. "What are you doing out here?"

"Well, Hank, you know me, I'm out here helping with the production of another movie. We're working hard to get this one ready for release next spring, but I think we'll be on time." It was clear that Ralph was excited about his work and was eager to tell me more.

"Yeah, this one is a war picture," he continued. "The movie is titled *In Harm's Way* and we have John Wayne, Kirk Douglas and Patricia Neal working with us on the set, so we are pretty sure it will be a hit." There was nothing I could say to match his enthusiasm, so I was quiet as he went on.

"As a matter of fact, Hank, I'll be working with "The Duke" all day today. We're staying here during production, so he and I will be coming back here to the hotel after work. At the end the day, we'll probably go up to the rooftop restaurant for dinner, relax and have a few drinks. Why don't you come on up and join us after the game? It would be great to spend some time together and I'm sure the Duke would be happy to meet you."

"I'll be there!" I accepted, without giving the matter a second thought. "Be watching for me, Ralph. I'll be coming up there to meet you as soon as I can get away from the stadium. *Who could turn down an invitation like that*?"

The view was breathtaking! The sun was sinking into the ocean, while the lights of the city sparkled below. It all marked the end of another beautiful day on the island. There wasn't enough time to fully appreciate the view as I rode upward on the hotel's glass-enclosed, exterior elevator. I stayed onboard with a few other guests as we passed the top floors, 28, 29 and 30 and finally stepped off at the last stop, the rooftop.

The maitre d' was about to inquire about my reservation when I noticed Ralph walking toward me. He had been watching for me, just as I had asked and spotted me as soon as I walked in.

"Over this way, Hank," he invited, waving for me to follow him. "We're happy that you could make it. We have a seat over here at our table waiting for you."

I trailed closely behind Ralph as he led me on a short walk around the tables, to a glassed-in area overlooking the ocean.

"Well, here we are, Hank, here's our spot," he said, taking the lead and motioning for me to grab the vacant chair. "But, before you take a seat, let me introduce you to my friend, The Duke, Mr. John Wayne."

"How do ya' do, Hank?" The Duke asked in his deep voice, rising from his chair to greet me. "It's a real pleasure to meet ya'there, fella'."

"Thank you, sir. It's a pleasure to meet you as well, " I responded, remembering the respectful courtesies I had been taught as a child. At 6'- 4", he towered over me for the brief time he was standing. I was captured by the sight of his broad shoulders and his stern and rugged face. Suddenly, I realized that the iconic character of so many great films actually did exist in real life.

"I understand that you're a catcher and that you've had quite a career to this point," he remarked, initiating a friendly conversation.

"Yeah, Duke, Hank here, has put in a lot of years in both the American and National Leagues," Ralph chimed in before I could answer.

The Duke took a glance at my hands as I moved the napkin from my plate and reached for my water. He seemed to study them even closer as I took a quick sip from the goblet. It was my Masonic ring that had caught his attention.

"I see that you are a traveling man," he noted, still focusing on my hands. This practiced means of recognition among brothers indicated to me that he, too, was a Mason.

"Yes, sir, that's right, and besides that, I've been through the hot sands."

Understanding my message, the Duke nodded in approval and responded, "I, too."

With that phrase, I had informed him that I was Shriner and learned that he was one, as well. Throughout this exchange, Ralph had sat quietly and patiently, peering at each of us as we spoke. Our conversation had put him adrift. He was as lost as a songbird at a tomcat meeting.

The Duke's next words were confusing even to me, but would come to have a much clearer meaning in the years to come.

"Mirth is King!" he announced.

There was a brief silence at the table. I had no reply to offer. I was utterly clueless, with no idea about the point he was trying to make.

"Well, you're right about that," I finally spoke up. "If you're not having a good time, then something's wrong."

While my well-meaning, but off-track response got a polite laugh, it signaled to both of us that, compared to the Duke, I had not yet traveled as far along the paths of Masonic membership. Nevertheless, I would learn later that by using the salutation, "Mirth is King," he identified himself as being of The Royal Order of Jesters, an advanced degree within the organization of Freemasonry, comprised of Shriners in good standing and attained by invitation only. Not long after my meeting with Mr. Wayne, I, too, would be accepted as a Jester and would remain within The Royal Order for many years until officially demitting my place in 2010.

While the filming of *In Harm's Way* was completed on schedule in the spring of 1965, the movie proved to be one of the year's also-rans, finishing as only a moderate success at the box office. However, in this, his final appearance in a black and white movie, John Wayne executed his role as U.S. Navy Captain Rock Torrey with the strength and boldness Americans had come to expect from him. Regardless of the character he played, his onscreen presence made movie-goers proud to be Americans and assured us that good would always triumph in the end. He had a special way of reminding us that we lived in the greatest country on earth.

Because of his private nature, the Duke never wanted matters involving his family and personal life to reach the news. To avoid publicizing his serious health issues, he permitted only a select few to know that he had been diagnosed with cancer just weeks before he arrived in Honolulu to start filming *In Harm's Way*. Nor did he give any outward indication that once production was finished, he was slated to undergo radical surgery for the removal of a diseased lung and four ribs. His courage was real.

Marion Morrison, better known as John Wayne, was as much of a hero in real life as he was on onscreen. In his later years he was known to be outspoken and controversial with his conservative political views, while carrying deep regrets for not doing more to defend America when the call went out. Yet, there is no denying his love for his country and his desire to strive toward what would best serve her. With his passing in 1979, America lost one of its truest heroes. He was a man who epitomized bravery, fairness and patriotism, not only in front of the cameras, but also in the way he lived his life.

With the Hawaii Islanders in 1964, I was about to turn 35 years old and that's much too old for a catcher to be fighting for a job.

PHOTO GALLERY

My father at an early age--he raised me to be a baseball player.

As a teenager, it was a thrill to meet one of the greatest players of all time, baseball legend George Sisler.

Photo from the front cover--Dodger speedster, Maury Wills is out at the plate. I applied the tag during the sixth inning at the L. A. Coliseum on Sept. 14, 1959. I was 2 for 4 in the game, with a homer and three RBI in a 4-3 win for the Pirates.

My first season as a pro: Manchester Yankees, 1948

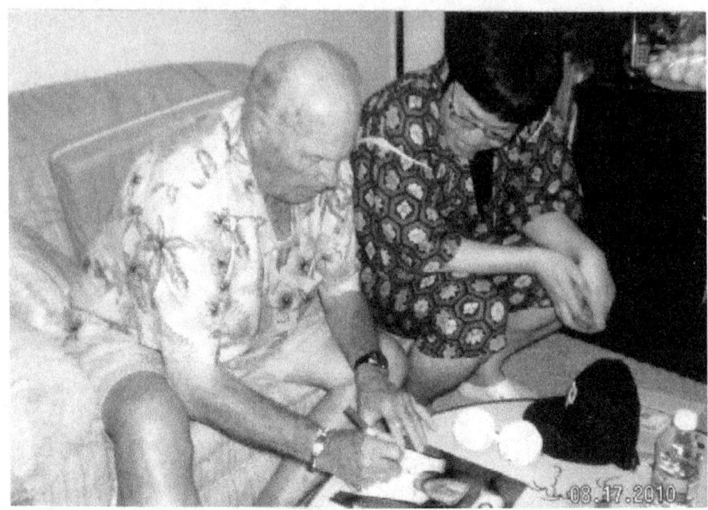

It's wonderful to have fans who live in other parts of the world. I finally met my friend, Kohei Nirengi, from Sano, Japan, while he was visiting in the United States in the summer of 2010. Kohei is a great baseball fan, collector and historian of the game.

Father and Son Day in Cincinnati was a special time, as I was joined on the field by Hank (left) and Marc.

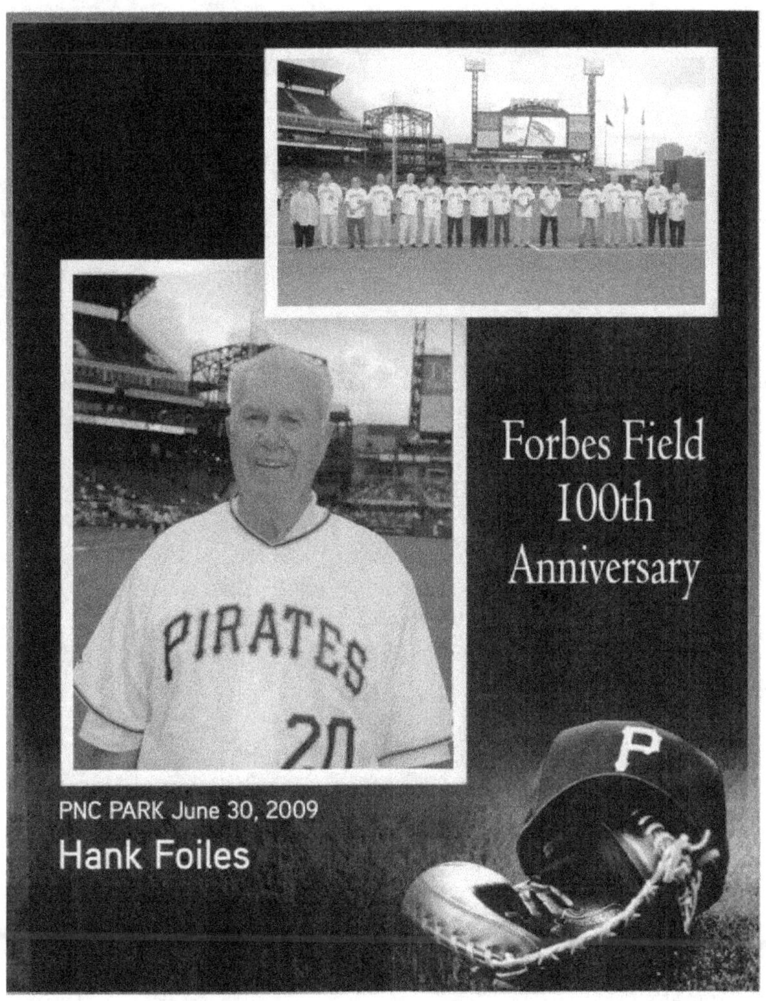

I was very pleased to be invited to the 100th Anniversary of Forbes Field in 2009. It was great to join so many of my Pirate friends at the new PNC Park in Pittsburgh. I was also honored to get behind the plate once again to catch the ceremonial first pitch, thrown by my old teammate, Elroy Face. What a grand occasion!

All dressed up--Joyce and I are joined by two other Pirate couples, Mr. and Mrs. Danny Kravitz (center) and Mr. and Mrs. Bob Porterfield (right) as we leave for a banquet given for the 1958 Pirates by the Westinghouse Broadcasting Co.

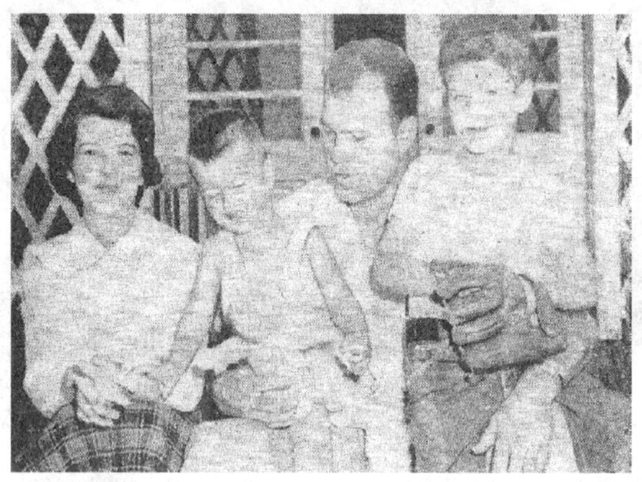

Pittsburgh was just one of the places Joyce and I called home during my career. That's Marc in the middle and Hank (right) with his baseball glove.

You can't make the club in the tub! I had a tough time with injuries and this sign in the Pirates' clubhouse summed up the situation.

May 3, 1955-- Because of his untimely death, my father saw me play in only one major league game. I was the Indians' starting catcher that day and went 2 for 3 at the plate in a 7-4 win over the Yankees. I scored on this close play in the seventh inning with a hard slide that jolted the ball out of the mitt of Yankee catcher, Yogi Berra.

Getting into shape-- Yankees' spring training, 1948. That's me, Ralph Houk, Jack Phillips and Mickey Witek (l-r).